Advance Prai
A Baptist Preacher's Bu

This beautifully written memoir is a testament to the power of the inward journey toward existential discovery, a pursuit too often impeded by social barriers. Universal and immanent, truth beckons to us beyond the boundaries of geography, nomenclature, or faith tradition. It will draw us nearer, Carter teaches, if only we muster the intellectual courage to let it light our path.

—**LARRY O. RIVERS,** Associate Professor of History,
University of West Georgia

A Baptist Preacher's Buddhist Teacher is a fascinating and provocative memoir, an honest, courageous, and moving account of a gentle and sensitive soul in a black male body in a black world, coming of age in one of the most fraught eras of US social-political unrest, especially racial conflicts. It shows readers what may be made of the persistent quest for more complex questioning and thinking, including efforts to press the religious life into service as fulcrum for healthy and courageous openness to and engagement and translation of different religious orientations for the sake of self-illumination and global social-political transformation. Carter's story should inspire and disturb all of us as it challenges our cherished and comforting assumptions, our tightly held claims and possessions, our glib tropes, including those about home, race, religion, self.

—**VINCENT L. WIMBUSH,** Director, Institute
for Signifying Scriptures

A Baptist
Preacher's
Buddhist
Teacher

A Baptist Preacher's Buddhist Teacher

*How My Interfaith Journey With
Daisaku Ikeda Made Me a Better Christian*

LAWRENCE EDWARD CARTER SR.

MIDDLEWAY
PRESS

Published by Middleway Press
A division of the SGI-USA
606 Wilshire Blvd.
Santa Monica, CA 90401

Cover and interior design by *the*BookDesigners

22 21 20 19 18   1 2 3 4 5

ISBN: 978-0-9779245-9-2

Library of Congress Cataloging-in-Publication Data

Names: Carter, Lawrence Edward, 1941- author.
Title: A Baptist peacher's Buddhist teacher : how my interfaith journey with
   Daisaku Ikeda made me a better Christian / Lawrence Edward Carter Sr.
Description: Santa Monica, CA : Middleway Press, 2018. | Includes
   bibliographical references.
Identifiers: LCCN 2018012798| ISBN 9780977924592 (trade paper : alk.
paper) |
   ISBN 9781946635068 (epub) | ISBN 9781946635075 (mobi)
Subjects: LCSH: Christianity and other religions--Buddhism. |
   Buddhism--Relations--Christianity. | Carter, Lawrence Edward, 1941- |
   Ikeda, Daisaku.
Classification: LCC BR128.B8 C375 2018 | DDC 261.2/43092--dc23
LC record available at https://lccn.loc.gov/2018012798

To

Howard Washington Thurman,
who worked as if the walls did not exist,

and

Robert Cummings Neville,
who understands the importance of a global,
sacred philosophy for our little blue planet

and

Martin Luther King Jr.,
who said Jesus led him to Gandhi

Table of Contents

Preface

I am writing on the Fourth of July at my home in Stonecrest, Georgia. The staccato sounds of firecrackers celebrating American independence echo in the distance. The notion of freedom is in my consciousness.

The Baptist Church of which I am a lifelong member has a tenet of faith called "freedom of conscience." This means that members are free to work out their own soul's salvation. Hence, they are free to practice their original way of being a Christian. There is no such thing as a pure Baptist. In fact, we must always hold our beliefs and convictions with a tentative confidence—a willingness to say good riddance to limiting perspectives and to move beyond dogmatic small-mindedness. This does not mean we abandon our core beliefs and convictions but that we are called to widen our perception of the world and enlarge our understanding of who we really are.

Martin Luther King Jr., one of the most famous Baptists of the twentieth century, says: "I can never be what I ought to be until you are what you ought to be. You can never be what you ought to be until I am what I ought to be. . . . This is the interrelated structure of reality."[1] There is at the heart of Baptist spirituality a moral imperative to be concerned about the so-called others and, in the process of respecting everybody's humanity, to be prepared with openness to learn from everybody—in spite of our seeming differences.

There are people who don't want to embrace new philosophies, and they don't want to move beyond narrow allegiances. But I believe it makes me more of a Christian to be able to relate to diverse peoples. We are called to embody "Christ" consciousness and to have a love big enough to embrace the world. All people are our brothers and sisters, irrespective of their particulars. We are not free unless every person is free. This kind of identification with all of humanity is the religion of Jesus. Jesus said, "And I have other sheep, that are not of this fold; I must bring them also."[2]

There are basically two ways for a religious practitioner—or, at least, this is so in Christianity—to engage with religious practitioners who are just as dedicated to their faith as Christians are to theirs. One has been to convert them. The other has been to respectfully learn from them and to seek not unity but harmony.

There is an old African proverb from Uganda: "He who never visits thinks his mother is the best cook."

My interfaith journey with Daisaku Ikeda seeking spiritual resources is not new. The Hindu Mohandus K. Gandhi was mentored by a Russian nonviolent pacifist, Leo Tolstoy, who believed that Christian, Buddhist, and Hindu renunciation was the true path to holiness. Martin Luther King Jr. said Jesus led him to Gandhi, and Nelson Mandela employed Gandhian nonviolence and civil disobedience to address social injustice in South Africa. Daisaku Ikeda has traveled all over the planet to have dialogues about peace with people of diverse backgrounds. These leaders explored other religious traditions for the means and mechanisms to bring about cross-cultural transformation and cosmopolitan democracy. They were willing to leave home and look beyond their own backyard.

Gandhi never renounced his Hinduism, but he claimed to be a follower of Jesus. He read the religions of the world and adopted many of their prayers, hymns, and rituals. He even prayed the Nichiren Buddhist chant practiced by Ikeda's Soka Gakkai International. King was a trained Christian theologian. But just because he had a PhD, he didn't quit growing. He got to know his brothers and sisters beyond Georgia, and beyond the United States—and he found common cause with people all around the world who were suffering. Reading Tolstoy did not make Gandhi less of a Hindu. Reading Gandhi did not make King less of a Christian. Nor have my conversations with Daisaku Ikeda made me less of a Baptist. Instead, they have given me a deeper understanding of my own faith.

Daisaku Ikeda models, for me, what it means to be a cosmic citizen. He has dialogued with ambassadors, anthropologists, economists, educators, historians, journalists, jurists, linguists, political statesmen, scientists, social engineers, sociologists, theologians, and urban planners—and he spoke with me and changed my life.

Mahatma Gandhi said: "I do not want my house to be walled in on all sides and my windows to be stuffed. I want the culture of all lands to be blown about my house as freely as possible. But I refuse to be blown off my feet by any."[3]

I intend to open all the windows of my house and, without getting blown off my feet, let the cultural winds of the world blow through. We can widen our perception of the world and enlarge our understanding of who we are, what we are capable of, what we ought to envision, in solidarity with others.

When I met Daisaku Ikeda, I understood at last the possibility of realizing Martin Luther King's utopian vision of the world house. It wasn't a dream anymore. It could be a reality.

"A utopia shatters a given order; and it is only when it starts shattering order that it is a utopia. A utopia is then always in the process of being realized."

—Paul Ricoeur

Acknowledgments

Nothing is self-made. All have parents, guardians, progenitors, supporters, critics, and teachers who help perfect one's craft. Writing is a discipline that requires time, focus, honesty, meditation, reflection, patience, research, debate, redefinition, and revisions. Without this process, you will never discover what you believe. Writing helps to clarify and refine your position on issues affecting common humanity.

Robert M. Franklin made it possible for me to expand the chapel staff. Quentin Samuels was my professional researcher and proofreader. Michael Bernard Beckwith, Rickie Byars Beckwith, Anne Fields Ford, Danny Nagashima, Daniel Y. Habuki, Ian McIllraith, Louis A. Nieves, Congdon Saita Smith, Clifford Sawyer, Renu Debozi, Charlise Lyles, Richard Brown, Willis B. Sheftall Jr., Harold V. Bennett, George David Miller, Neelakanta Radhakrishnan, Sri Sri Ravi Shankar, and Daisaku Ikeda are my moral, spiritual, and significant supporters. Dave McNeill of Middleway Press has kept this project alive. The dedicated Martin Luther King Jr. International Chapel staff—including Terry and Donna Walker, Adrienne Harris, Jane J. Jones, Eric Richards, John Jordan, Khalfani Lawson, Tiant Holloway, Jordan Muckey, and Marissa Clay—have supported me in so many ways so that I could complete this project. Gratitude is owed to them as well as to Clark Strand, Perdita Finn, and Earle Clowney for their editorial expertise.

Special gratitude goes to Dr. John R. Silber, who first hired me to head the Martin Luther King Jr. African American Cultural Center and to be associate dean at Marsh Chapel at Boston University; Dr. Hugh M. Gloster Sr., president of Morehouse College, who hired me in 1979; and Dr. David A. Thomas, the current president, who has greatly freed me to pursue my scholarship and work on this book. I'm deeply grateful for the generous endorsements of Robert C. Neville, Lewis V. Baldwin, Larry O. Rivers, Vincent L. Wimbush, and especially Echol Nix Jr., the editor of a festschrift in my honor, *In the Beginning: The Martin Luther King Jr. International Chapel at Morehouse College.*

My mother, Bernice Carter Johnson, and my aunt, Eddie Kate Mays, and their mother, Willie Childs Mullins, were the most powerful and influential personalities in my formative years. They are responsible for my pastoral caring spirit. My pastors, Jacob Ashburn and Jacob Julian Ashburn, taught me the gospel of Jesus Christ.

My greatest cheerleaders in all of my endeavors are my wife of forty-nine years and my best conversational partner and revisionist, Dr. Marva Griffin Carter, and our son, Lawrence Edward Carter Jr. For their unconditional help and love, I am eternally grateful.

Chapter One

Getting the Call

In the waning years of the twentieth century, I found myself in a state of deep disappointment. It was more than millennial malaise; it was inconsolable despair. Day after day, I worked tirelessly at my desk in a small, book-lined office as the founding dean of the Martin Luther King Jr. International Chapel at Morehouse College in Atlanta. For the thirty or so years since King's death, I had been striving to realize his vision for equality, justice, and peace—both at his alma mater and in the wider world.

I had designed and implemented a range of courses, workshops, conferences, and exchanges trying to instill a progressive Christian consciousness within my students, many of them pastors, theologians, ethicists, Biblical scholars, engineers, philosophers-in-training preparing to go out into the world to preach the Gospel. Out of all my endeavors, all my toils, the students of Morehouse College have been my most valued and lasting contribution.

Still, I felt grief at all that I had yet to accomplish. Attendance at Sunday morning and evening King Chapel services remained meager in the Crown Nave. When I had accepted the deanship of the brand new King Chapel, Morehouse president emeritus Benjamin E. Mays had said to me, "If you can consistently fill the Sunday morning chapel service with five hundred people, you will have triumphed." After three decades in the chapel, I had not triumphed.

A powerful choir had failed to consistently develop into an inimitable vocal force. A substantial and highly skilled staff to manage the chapel had yet to be assembled. So many of my sermons had fallen short of the thunderous, inspirational preaching that I dreamed might shake the halls of Christendom and government. And when my sermon preparation exceeded my expectations on some Sundays, few students were in the congregation and no faculty members were there to hear my effort or to participate in the sermon talk-backs after the services. All this even though Hugh M. Gloster, who hired me, thought that I was exceptional and never missed an opportunity to affirm my work. He even wanted me to succeed him as president of Morehouse College. But when Thomas Kilgore Jr., chairman of the board of trustees, asked me if I wanted to be president in 1987, I thought about it briefly and said no.

So many projects remained unfunded. So many books were still unwritten and unpublished. Portraits of seminal figures remained unpainted for the chapel's International Hall of Honor for civil and human rights leaders.

The world house that my mentor Martin Luther King Jr. dreamed of was still unconstructed. Toward the end of his final book, *Where Do We Go From Here?: Chaos or*

Community, published in 1967, King wrote, "We have inherited a large house, a great 'world house' in which we have to live together—black and white, Easterner and Westerner, Gentile and Jew, Catholic and Protestant, Moslem and Hindu, Buddhist and Bedouin—a family unduly separated in ideas, culture and interest, who, because we can never again live apart, must learn somehow to live with each other in peace."[4]

Throughout the last year of his life, King consistently spoke of this world house, saying how small the world had become, how the jet plane and television had shrunk the planet. And what was true in 1968 would only become more true—with cell phones, the internet, and the migration of people around the globe. Even then, King cautioned against the separation and segregation of people within nation-state boundaries. Certainly, current world issues like the "war on terror," the global economic crisis, the refugee crisis, immigrant rights, nuclear weapons, and global warming have only made his observations more acute and necessary today.

By speaking about the world house, King had begun to speak of civil and human rights from a global, even cosmic, perspective, connecting the American nonviolent Civil Rights Movement to a critique of colonialism and war and our treatment of Earth and outer space. Many responded by saying that he should confine the scope of his work to ending the segregation of the American South, and among these critics were people who considered themselves to be his followers. But he would not do it. He could not. He was a visionary who championed the struggle to realize a

sustainable world where people ought to live free of violence and injustice.

As an African American man whose only arsenal was
a briefcase of speeches about ethics, justice, nonviolence,
sustainability, cosmopolitan discourse, and cosmic companionship, I often felt that my commitment to peace was
not taken seriously enough by my academic and Christian
colleagues, many of whom seemed more interested in ceremonial and token acknowledgments of King as opposed
to building creative and effective activism for justice and
social policy changes. Indeed, I sensed that many of them
thought that, with his talk of peace, Dr. Lawrence Edward
Carter Sr. was just another useless Pollyanna.

In the decades since my mentor's assassination, I
watched as America and the world stumbled blindly, seemingly mindlessly, into ever-increasing cultures of conflict
and confusion. From the violence that permeates our entertainment, to domestic violence in our homes, to assault-
weapon wielding sociopaths and street gangs, to disrespect
and intransigence in the halls of our government, to pro-
tracted armed animosities between nations, to genocidal
wars around the world, to the threat of nuclear confron-
tation and the very destruction of our species and our
planet—we behave as if violence is the primary purpose of
humankind on Earth.

What was I doing to make a difference? As men in late
middle age tend to do, I weighed myself on Daniel's prover-
bial and unforgiving scales and found myself wanting: as a

Christian minister trying to practice the religion of Jesus, as a teacher, as the curator of an institution that stood at the epicenter of American Civil Rights and world human rights, and, most significantly, as a disciple of Martin Luther King Jr., a man I had known and embraced as my mentor.

The year was 1999. I remember it was a beautiful day, warm, like summer. It was quiet around the chapel. The students were gone. The phone rang and it was a member of the Morehouse alumni clergy and a very dear friend of mine, Amos C. Brown, the pastor of the nation's oldest African American church west of the Mississippi River, San Francisco's Third Baptist Church.

"Are you watching the news?" he asked urgently, as soon as I picked up.

"Yes . . ."

"Are you aware of what has happened in Colorado? At Columbine High School?"

"Yes." I sighed. The news of the mass shooting by adolescent boys killing their classmates and teachers weighed heavy on me.

But before I could express my thoughts, Amos interrupted me: "What are you going to do about it?"

The question startled me. I had not thought about my personal responsibility in this instance. Long after the call was over I sat in my office, haunted by this question. What was I going to do about all the violence in the world? What was I personally going to do about Columbine?

It was really a question for Martin Luther King Jr.

himself. What would he have wanted me to do? I thought of his mentor Mohandas K. Gandhi, whose life, work, and writing I have studied with great intensity, making him my mentor for peace too. The words of King kept playing over and over in my head and in my heart: "We must all learn to live together as brothers or we will all perish together as fools. We are tied together in the single garment of destiny, caught in an inescapable network of mutuality" and "It is no longer a choice, my friends, between violence and nonviolence. It is either nonviolence or nonexistence."

I was responsible. What was I going to do?

I could hear Gandhi and King telling me that sustained, nonviolent resolution to conflict can be achieved. I saw before me the blueprint and the tools they had left behind to make peaceful coexistence real on the planet, but something felt like it was missing. No matter how desperately I held to my mentors' vision, I still felt I had made little or no progress in creating real momentum around peace as a living, breathing way of being in the world, a real and living possibility in the minds of my students and my small, ever-changing Sunday congregation at the chapel, my Morehouse colleagues and fellow clergy. In truth, I felt I had done nothing toward creating a sustainable culture of peace.

Yet I had great confidence in that blueprint for living nonviolently. If only I could get that blueprint in front of ordinary people everywhere—be they migrant workers, custodians or teachers, corporate executives, political leaders, diplomats, or heads of nations. I wanted to present

Mahatma Gandhi and Martin Luther King Jr. as role models for peace and highlight the ideas and practices that make a life of nonviolence and peaceful coexistence possible. I wanted to plant those practices in people's daily lives and keep them alive and active by studying, practicing, and promoting them. At the time, Gandhi and King were my sole focus. I had not yet realized that I might have another mentor, whose authentic practice of nonviolence would approach the spiritual caliber of Gandhi and King. I had not thought of looking beyond Hinduism and Christianity, even though Gandhi had said that the roots of nonviolence could be found not only in Hinduism and Christianity but in Buddhism and Islam as well.

Sitting alone in my office, I made the decision to have what I called a Millennium Sunday. I wanted to claim Gandhian principles of nonviolence, and I wanted to claim King's philosophical nonviolence but merge them in an entirely new way, as I was under the impression that no one had done this significantly in this country. As the dean of the Martin Luther King Jr. International Chapel at King's alma mater, I knew we were the most prominent religious memorial to him and that I was the one to do this, not just for Morehouse or even Atlanta but for the nation and the world.

I began by looking at what a Millennium Sunday would be and who would be involved. I chose April 2, 2000, and I talked with people in our communications office about it. They wrote a press release for the newspaper explaining Millennium Sunday and the founding of the Gandhi

Institute for Reconciliation at King Chapel. But when the phone rang a few days later, I had no idea that this had been done.

I was completely surprised when the woman on the other end of the telephone said: "Hi, I'm Ann Fields Ford. I'm a professor of social work across the street at Clark Atlanta University. Have you seen the newspaper?"

When I told her I had not, she said, "There is an article indicating you are going to do peace work."

I had not thought of it exactly in those terms, but as I sat in silence thinking, I realized that she was right. "Yes, I guess I am," I answered.

"Do you know who Daisaku Ikeda is?" she asked.

I did not.

I have always believed you have to get out of your comfort zone, beyond the Mason-Dixon Line in your mind. If a nonviolent consciousness and peace activism are to take hold in the United States and around the world, we first need to open our hearts and minds to new influences and to truth, irrespective of its origins. This is something I believe King learned from his own mentor, Morehouse president Benjamin E. Mays, whose master's thesis at the University of Chicago was on how Christianity drew from various pagan practices. Mays said anyone who disputed this simply had not done their homework.

As a follower of Jesus, I have sought to study the beliefs, philosophies, and practices of myriad religions and spiritual leaders. Indeed, I have opened the pulpit of King Chapel to leaders of every religious faith from Catholicism to Islam, Sikhs to Protestants, Judaism to Hinduism. I have hosted speakers as diverse as the liberal theologian Matthew Fox and the noted rabbi Michael Lerner. I have welcomed the ideas of imams, innovators, pagans, scientists, and spiritual seekers of all kinds. As a black ordained American Baptist minister, I pride myself on broad-mindedness and an eagerness to explore religious scriptures and practices quite different from my own. I have read the writings of everyone from black liberationist theologian James Cone to philosophical theologians Robert Cummings Neville and Paul Tillich to French Jesuit mystical paleontologist Pierre Teilhard de Chardin to Polish American Jewish philosopher and rabbi Abraham Joshua Heschel to New Thought Ancient Wisdom mystics Ernest Holmes, Eckhart Tolle, and Wayne Dyer to native South Korean cosmopolitan theologian Namsoon Kang to Buddhist meditation master and Vietnamese monk and peace activist Thich Nhat Hanh to British Indian philosopher Jiddu Krishnamurti to Greek-born evolutionary biologist Elisabet Sahtouris and American theoretical quantum physicist Fred Alan Wolf. But I had never heard of this man Daisaku Ikeda. He was completely unknown to me until that morning.

In less than fifteen minutes, Ann Fields Ford was in the chapel library. I heard this woman say: "Wow! This is the biggest secret in the Atlanta University Center Consortium." She was completely surprised and arrested to discover the large collection of enlarged historic framed and unframed photographs that cover nearly every square inch of the walls from the floor to the ceiling in the large chapel library, photographs that document the widely held belief that Morehouse College is the school that started the American nonviolent Civil and Human Rights Movement.

I stuck my head out of my office door and there she was—a confident, middle-aged, African American PhD in social work, a fellow academic across the street at Clark Atlanta University whom I somehow had never met. She introduced herself as a member of the Soka Gakkai International-USA, a lay Nichiren Buddhist organization with a chapter here in Atlanta.

We sat down at the conference table in the library, and Ann explained to me that the Soka Gakkai International's president, Daisaku Ikeda, was her mentor in faith. Since 1960, he had led an international peace movement born largely out of the August 1945 atomic bombings of Hiroshima and Nagasaki. The SGI had since grown to a membership of twelve million practitioners in 192 countries and territories. She told me that this Buddhist spiritual teacher was active in other realms as well: he was an educator who had founded two world-class universities and an international school system from kindergarten through high school, and he was a peace activist who had long been involved at the international level advocating peace, nuclear disarmament, and human rights education. To say the least, I was embarrassed. As a trained clinical theologian and professor of religion, I felt I should have known about Daisaku Ikeda, the practice of Nichiren Buddhism, and the Soka Gakkai International.

Ann brought me a hardback copy of *Choose Life: A Dialogue* by Arnold Toynbee and Daisaku Ikeda. After she had gone, I picked it up, intending only to skim it. But I was immediately drawn in by Ikeda's eloquence and the clear and informative way he articulated his thoughts with eruditeness about political and economic issues from a perspective of spirituality. I was truly inspired by his message that the key to social change was a profound inner spiritual reformation—an inner revolution and integrity of character. I was ready to learn more about him and his international organization. But I was surprised and wonderfully impressed when I discovered Ikeda's interdisciplinary grasp of the connection between economic growth and war. This sophisticated understanding of social issues from the perspective of Ikeda's Buddhist faith put him, for me, in the tradition of Gandhi and King's prophetic socialized spirituality. Ikeda said to Toynbee, professor emeritus of history at the University of London:

The nature of war has been described as an armed version of politics and diplomacy, but while politics today remains a partial cause, economic factors seem to play a larger role in warfare and military preparations. The problem of abolishing warfare requires study from many angles; there are many causative elements behind the necessity for nations to expend vast parts of their budgets on war. But under current conditions, the most important problem is devising a way to secure economic prosperity while avoiding confrontations that might lead to warfare. . . .

War is undeniably an evil and a danger to the dignity of life. Equally undeniable, however, is the stimulation war has given to economic and technological development. In the modern world, war and preparation for it seem to be deeply related to economic needs. At any rate, war is a way of disposing of surpluses in the immense industrial productive power of our society. In a state of emergency, all resources of a country are mobilized; war takes precedence over everything. Activities of society are controlled and systematized for the purposes of war and reorganized in their most rational and effective forms for the final goal of victory. At such times, strength unimaginable under ordinary conditions is added to the general effort.

Under the impetus of the two world wars, aircraft, rockets, and atomic power were rapidly researched and developed. After the wars ended, peaceful uses brought blessings to mankind. By increasing demand and the need for labor, war and war preparations play an important role in stabilizing economic development, but a kind of repetitive cycle is established in which vast economies bring about wars and wars stimulate further economic growth. . . .

War now threatens our civilization and our continued existence on this globe. We ought to do something to alter the basic nature of economics so that it no longer stimulates warfare. There are a number of factors aside from war that can promote economic growth. For instance, expanding and improving our social security and educational systems, providing better housing for our people, and giving massive foreign aid to underdeveloped countries would demand sums sufficiently vast to support the economies of most nations.[5]

Less than a week later, Ann assembled a group of SGI members at my office, with Morehouse students among them. I had not even known the SGI was represented in our student body. A local lawyer, Richard Brown, who later became a judge, presided over the meeting and brought me many more books by Ikeda. Everyone introduced themselves: Richard Brown, Quan Sullivan, Brad Yeates, Anne Fields Ford, Donna Fabian, and others. Richard was making a few statements about the SGI, when I stopped everything.[6]

"Wait a minute, wait a minute, time out," I said, a little surprised. "What's the motive here? What do you really want?" I could tell that they were negotiating for something.

"We want you to establish an SGI club or society at Morehouse or the Atlanta University Center."

"You've got it," I said. After all, the Catholics have Newman House, the Episcopalians have Canterbury House, and the Jews have Hillel House in the academy. "We'd love to welcome the Buddhists."

Everyone seemed pleased and started telling me more

about Ikeda. I learned that when he became president of the group, it existed only in Japan and that he had internationalized it. He only spoke one language, but still he traveled around the world and had dialogues with different leaders. He did not let language or race or disciplinary boundaries or national borders or religion deter him. He sallied forth.

One of the young people mentioned *kosen-rufu*, and I stopped him. "What does that mean?"

"Global peace. Daisaku Ikeda's goal is a commonwealth of global citizens."

"You mean a beloved world community that transcends internationalism?" I said, paraphrasing King.

The young man smiled. That rang true.

I realized in that instant that Ikeda's vision was in the very process of realization and was no different from Martin Luther King Jr.'s vision of the world house. I could offer them a campus organization. But perhaps the Soka Gakkai could offer me something as well: that missing piece of King and Gandhi's blueprint for a world without violence.

"I'm sensing a great deal of connectedness between Ikeda, King, and Gandhi," I said, "and the more I read, I am beginning to see they were all about the same thing. All three ultimately talked about the world community, a cosmopolitan utopia of equity for all and how we achieve that. Martin Luther King denounced injustice anywhere as a threat to justice everywhere. As he wrote: "I must constantly respond to the Macedonian call for aid. . . . I cannot sit idly by in Atlanta and not be concerned about what happens in Birmingham."[7] This is King's most succinct definition of himself as a moral cosmopolitan.

I had been called first by my prophetic friend Amos Brown asking me what I was going to do about Columbine and now again by the SGI.

Martin Luther King Jr. emphasized that we are all involved in a "network of mutuality," a "single garment of destiny," and Ikeda talks about the interconnectedness of everything, "codependent origination," the inseparability of life. It echoes in South Africa's *ubuntu*: "I am because we are." The whole Nichiren chant, Nam-myoho-renge-kyo, which literally means "devotion to the Lotus Sutra of the Wonderful Law," is connected to this human interwovenness and the inherent dignity of every human being—what Martin Luther King refers to as the sacredness of all human personality. This transcends nationalism and is cosmopolitan in every respect. It transcends all boundaries and it takes precedent over militarily enforced sovereign government policies. So when people are hurting we are obligated to be of assistance to them any- and everywhere in the world.

The internet has now become the nervous system of the planet. Distant wars are fought in our living room. Hence, we cannot know and not know what is happening around the planet. If we are going to practice virtue ethics, we are going to have to be guided by principles that help us evaluate, obligate, universalize, affirm, cooperate, and sustain. Without all this, there can be no justice. We sit before the merciless glare of television every evening to hear the news on all the networks. And it's all about human need and what ought to be on our prayer list. What's happening to people? What are we going to do?

Paraphrasing the German theologian Martin Niemoller, Angela Davis said that if they come for me in the morning and nobody says anything, and they come for your neighbors at noon and nobody says anything, when they come for you in the evening, there may not be anybody left to speak up.

Jet travel, cell phones, and all other forms of transport and communication make our planet much smaller, and for us to ignore what is happening to neighbors, locally or globally, is for us to ignore the teachings of Jesus, of Gandhi, of King, and now I realized, also of Daisaku Ikeda. The whole moral cosmopolitan idea is about identifying with global humanity, the cosmos, and never taking the attitude that the suffering of others is not relevant to me. Your address is much larger than you think. You are a cosmic citizen! The universe is your home! It's the whole Christian message. Now I was seeing that it was also the teaching of the SGI and Nichiren Buddhism.

Thus I embarked on a journey to understand the Soka Gakkai International, its president Daisaku Ikeda, and the *kosen-rufu* movement for peace through the spread of Nichiren Buddhist philosophy and practice of chanting the phrase Nam-myoho-renge-kyo. I realized that in the King Chapel International Hall of Honor oil portrait gallery, where I had hung the likenesses of civil and human rights leaders, and nonviolent practitioners of all faiths and nationalities, I had overlooked the work of a United Nations–recognized and honored peace activist.

I found Daisaku Ikeda's books and published peace proposals to the United Nations to be an insightful evolution of the nonviolent philosophies of both Gandhi and King.

For example, his 1982 classic, *Life: An Enigma, a Precious Jewel,* provides a more detailed, subtle, and profound analysis of the flow of cosmic life's eternal reality, its evolutionary emergence, and its connection to religious sentiment than any explanation known to me.

"Religion is, in effect, a more essential aspect of human life than intelligence, morality, or conscience," writes Ikeda. "Neither intelligence nor conscience can unlock the great door of life. The key to human existence is the inborn religious impulse that springs from and aspires to return to essential universal life. . . . The life force is omnipresent."[8]

I have often said that the heart of my theology is *eternal omnipresence.* Why? Because all Christian preachers preach on Acts 17:28: "In him we live and move and have our being." If that's true, then we are *in* God, not *under* God, as some American patriots say. And if we are *in* God—living, moving, and having our being—and God is eternal omnipresence, doesn't that also mean that every substance that God is—every virtue, every bit of wholeness, health, wealth, and harmony that God is—is right where we are, and we can tap into it. It is closer than our breath and our heartbeat because we are living and moving and having our being in God.

That's like saying, we are not born, and we do not die; we come from life, and we return to life. We appear, and we disappear. According to Ikeda, this omnipresent life force (which we Christians call God) underlies the so-called birth and death of all living phenomena. "Universal life was operating throughout the three-billion-year process required for the evolution of living creatures," Ikeda writes.[9] I take this as his interpretation of the six days of creation found in Genesis—a "day" being, in reality, billions and billions of years and therefore almost infinite. And where there is universal life on such a vast unfolding scale, according to Ikeda, there must also be religious sentiment and a continuing evolution—and the possibility for human revolution. We have always been here, and we always will be here, because as all of science tells us, energy cannot be destroyed. It only changes forms.

This and other insights that seemed to interpret core spiritual truths on a truly cosmic scale was what I found so impressive about Ikeda's writings as a modern philosopher. But the more I came to know about Ikeda, the more I was inspired by his accomplishments as a religious leader as well—as a cosmic citizen-scholar, a peace activist, and a pioneering educator engaged throughout the world in dialogical friendships. In studying his life and good works, I began feeling more confident of my own path as a follower of Jesus than ever before. My theological and liturgical vocabulary expanded, and my comfort level in the interfaith community grew exponentially.

It also became clear to me that there is great symmetry between the nontheistic philosophy of Nichiren Buddhism and the very theistic New Thought Ancient Wisdom tradition, best exemplified in the teachings of the United Church of Religious Science, Unity, and those other denominations most influenced by spiritual philosopher Ernest Holmes's 1926 mistitled book, *The Science of Mind*. Michael Bernard Beckwith of Los Angeles is currently the most internationally recognized independent teacher in this communion of cosmopolitan theology. My faith in the social teachings of Jesus and my knowledge of the mystical writings of Howard Thurman combined with the teachings of Beckwith and Holmes led me to Ikeda—just as King said Jesus led him to Mohandus K. Gandhi. Eventually I met Ikeda face to face and found him to be a profoundly authentic and humble person, spiritual genius that he obviously was.

It was on that very first day in 1999 when I was introduced to the SGI that I realized Daisaku Ikeda and I shared the same moral cosmopolitan cause—and I experienced my despair evaporating like the dew in a bright sun and felt, as Psalm 30 puts it, the joy that "cometh in the morning" with the start of a bright, new day.

Chapter Two

My Path

I have come to believe that the genesis of my own, and Ikeda's, intense commitment to global peace emanates from the agony of watching our mothers grieve over the losses of husbands and sons to the violence of World War II. The simple love of our mothers propelled our lifelong desire to extinguish the scourge of war and to see the human species dwell in peace.

My earliest memory is of hearing how my grandmother received the news that my uncle, her eldest son, Curtis Childs, had been killed at Pearl Harbor. She was on her way home from working all day in a white home in Dawson, Georgia, of Terrell County. It had already turned dark. As she approached the black part of town, where the unpaved streets started, she passed one of the few houses of the community in which there was a telephone. Her neighbor told her to come up on the porch and have a seat and rest awhile. My grandmother was totally unsuspecting of what she was about to hear.

The news of death for the black community in Dawson first arrived at the office of the mortician, Joe Moore Steward, on Main Street. He would then telephone the news to the side of town from which the receiver could most easily relay the information by word of mouth to the person who needed to hear it. My grandmother, Willie Mae Roberts Childs Mullins, was greatly fatigued that day, and her arms were full of groceries and laundry. She'd been working since sunrise. Her neighbor let her settle in and rest for a minute in the rocking chair before she told her that there was some bad news from the mortician. Her son Curtis had been killed at Pearl Harbor.

My grandmother's grief was uncontrollable. She had had three sons, and she would lose one to the war, one in a car accident, and a third at the age of twenty-six from a cerebral hemorrhage. She also received the news that her son-in-law, my father, John Henry Carter III, had been the victim of a hand grenade attack and was shell shocked. There are many ways that war devastates families. There are, of course, the many casualties of combat, but there are also injuries that, while not immediately fatal, end up destroying people. Even though my father returned alive, the war robbed me of him.

My father left to serve in World War II when my mother was still carrying me, so on the day I was born, my father was already in Europe. I know very little about what he experienced because I knew him only a short while. The man who went to war was a talented, strong, even brilliant man, but only the shell of that man returned.

My father was physically well, but emotionally and mentally he was damaged beyond repair. I do know that he saw his best friend blown up right in front of him. A hand grenade spewed his entrails and limbs all over my father, who found himself wiping the body parts of his best friend off of his uniform and his face. This is the grotesque truth of war that we do not see in sanitized television and newspaper reports.

From my mother's stories, I had a fond memory of my father as a kind, gentle man. My mother said he was a brilliant student, and she had high hopes for him as did my grandmother. He had talked about becoming a preacher like his own father, who had preached in a small country church. But when Dad returned from the war, the doctors told my mother that he was shell shocked, a condition we know today as post-traumatic stress disorder. Unable to work, he was in and out of the Chillicothe (Ohio) Veterans Hospital for most of my youth. When my mother visited him in the hospital, I as a child was not permitted to enter with her. I was always told to wait in a neighbor's car. My memories of this experience depress me still. I still feel the tears on my face and the yearning in my chest to see my father. It felt like I was being punished and I did not understand why.

His trauma was so severe that he did not live with our family while I was growing up. I can remember seeing my father only twice, the last time in 1960, when I was only eighteen years old. He walked into our backyard on the Hilltop in Columbus, Ohio, at 26 South Oakley Avenue on a hot summer day. I had just graduated from West High School and was anticipating college in Virginia that fall. I was thrilled to see him! He looked perfectly well. We did not know where he came from, how he got to our house, or where he went when he left. He kept referring to me as the baby! He spoke well, but he did not stay long. My mother and my aunt were quiet. But before Dad left, as suddenly as he had appeared, he told me that he loved me. My deep hunger for those words will not let me ever forget that historic day.

He was periodically judged fit for discharge, but he was never well enough to live for long outside of the hospital. He would be released but would eventually always have some kind of episode that would cause him to be hospitalized again. My father stayed with us at our home only one month that I can remember. Most of the time I did not even know when he was discharged. When he was released, he lived alone—an alcoholic, dependent on the care and services of other people. After he left the military, he was never able to hold a job consistently.

I never doubted that my father was a good man, intelligent and able. And yet, he was profoundly sad. I can only imagine what other unspoken horrors he experienced on the battlefield that he was unable to live with later. I can only imagine what it must have felt like to have ability and potential and never be able to express it again. He was never able to function as an independent or successful man, never able to live up to his promise. And I am pained that he was never able to be a father to me. He never met my wife or son. I was informed by a Pentagon military historian just recently by telephone that my father had died in 1998. Why I was not notified earlier is beyond my comprehension.

A military nurse called our home in Decatur, Georgia, about 1991, when our son, Carter, was six years old. She confirmed my identity and informed me that my father wanted to speak with me. My first unuttered thought was "I am going to bring him to live with us!" But immediately, as if she were reading my mind, the nurse said: "It is not a good idea for you to invite your father to your home or for you to visit him. His coming to Georgia would have a bad effect on your family. He would be dependent. That could disrupt your house. I am going to put him on the phone to speak with you, but do not tell him that he can come to Georgia when he asks." Dad was very polite, and there were tender moments. I let my wife, Marva, and Carter speak with him and then the nurse ended the call after a while. I am so thankful that I got to hear his voice one last time.

There are people all around the world filled with such disappointment, so I am not alone. I have suffered losses, as so many of us have, and as Daisaku Ikeda has as well.

One of Ikeda's friends from his youth remembers that Daisaku would often say, "Life is vital," and then ask, in dead earnestness, during those battle-filled days, "What will the war do to us?"[10]

Life, indeed, is vital, and nothing destroys life or what is beautiful in it more savagely and on such a large scale as war. "Nothing is more barbarous than war," Ikeda would later write as the first lines to his novel *The Human Revolution*. "Nothing is more cruel."

That is why I hate war, because it robbed me of having my father in my life the way he wanted to be, and because it robbed my father of the possibility of realizing his fullest potential. There may be occasions where war seems justified, or even necessary. But whenever discussions occur about the advisability of sending young people into combat, no matter how just the cause, I cannot help considering the cost to their lives and their families.

I saw how my mother struggled as a result of losing her husband. My mother raised me as a single parent, laboring at three, sometimes four jobs, having to work harder than she should have because war had reduced her husband to a dependent alcoholic. I watched my mother do heavy manual labor late into the evening, working in dark, shuttered factories, alone with a big buffer in her hands. Naive, I once accompanied her to assist but found the labor too strenuous for my weak grade-school hands, even later when I was in college.

My mother sought work in Columbus, Ohio, because Negroes could not always get work in the American South. When she moved to establish herself in a new place, she had to leave me with my maternal grandmother in Georgia, where I lived until I was five when my grandmother died in 1946.

My grandmother's house was on an unpaved street, a red clay road with a bit of sand that separated it from our property. The house rested on brick stilts. When you looked down at the floor, you could see holes and see the ground.

And when you looked up at the ceiling, a tin roof, you could see holes and see the sky. There was no electricity, no running water, no inside toilet. We cooked on a stove that burned wood. That was the house in which I was born at 417 South Walnut Street in Dawson, Georgia.

One day when I was just a little kid with short pants and bare feet, I was standing in the front yard with my puppy, Benny, a friendly chocolate Labrador retriever. It was a Saturday afternoon, and I heard my grandmother say: "Lawrence Edward, get Benny out of the yard and get him in the house! Do that right now."

I remember doing just that, not knowing what was going on. But as I was making my moves, I looked up the street to see three white men walking right down the middle of it with rifles in their hands. I had never seen guns before, although I knew they existed. I stopped to watch, stunned by what I was seeing. The men aimed their guns right at one of the nearby homes and started shooting! I was trying to figure out what they were shooting at and then it became clear. I heard a dog yelping, barking, and screaming.

I had no idea what was happening. I just heard the shots. And I heard the animals screaming in pain. By the time they arrived at my house, Benny was inside and so was I. I peeked out the window and they walked right by. Madear, as I affectionately called her, explained, "They're killing dogs that do not have licenses." That was the first time I associated violence with white people and understood the gap in value between black property and white property.

There are many ways to view violence. It repels and alarms us, but it also attracts and entertains us. It destroys us, but it can protect us too—or at least we think it can. People want to make other persons serve their interests or take something from them or make them conform. But the essential quality of violence is more than physical coercion or force. Violence is, finally, whether expressed in action or in words, the complete degradation of life.

The use of physical force against others is just one expression of violence. The mere threat of bodily harm can also be coercive and damaging. We can deny another's humanity with words as our only weapons.

That kind of violence—of language, behavior, insinuation—is often the hardest to spot and the hardest to restrain. Even though we may not regard ourselves as violent people, we may speak hurtful words more often than we realize and usually feel we have good reason. And yet, as both Mahatma Gandhi and Martin Luther King Jr. articulated many times, the perpetrators of violence are also diminished and damaged by their actions.

I experienced the violence of segregation and discrimination very early. One night there was great excitement in Dawson when a minstrel show came to town. We went over to Main Street, which was paved, past my Uncle Mud's grocery store, to the baseball field where a stage had been erected. A lot of chairs had been set up, divided right down the middle by a rope. One side was for colored people, and the other side was for whites.

We were not there so much for the entertainment, which was white persons in blackface, as for the commercials, especially for the tonics that were on sale that were supposed to be a cure for everything. But the biggest illness those tonics couldn't fix was that rope dividing us from one another. I was sitting on the aisle, and for the entire show I could not stop staring at the white folks. Why was that rope there? I was sitting there, and I was younger than ten, and already I was thinking that these people were just like us and that one day I was gonna tear down that rope.

In 1952, when I was in the fifth grade, my family stepped over the rope. I was with my mother in Ohio by then, and we moved from an all-black neighborhood in Columbus on the east side of town to a racially mixed community on the west side, which we thought was better, to an area known as the Hilltop. We had a little front lawn with a larger yard in the back that I mowed and where I planted maple and oak trees. I took great pride in making that lawn look attractive. I guess I felt that I had something to prove. I wanted our neighbors to see that we belonged. We were black, but we could keep our lawn looking as nice as anyone. But my efforts at my home did not earn me respect at my school. And the sad truth was, I did not get the opportunities I longed to have.

To understand this, you have to appreciate what it was like for me as a young black child in America in the 1950s to have a dark complexion. I am a dark-skinned African American man with kinky hair and a natural gap between my two front teeth, which is a trait of certain African tribes, and I grew up during a time when lighter skin was seen as preferable, even among black folk.

Before Malcolm X and the Black Power movement, before we cried out that "Black is beautiful and it is beautiful to be black," or celebrated our color in the Black Arts Movement, before Nina Simone sang "To Be Young, Gifted, and Black," or before James Brown sang the words "Say it loud, I'm black and I'm proud," and certainly, long before, Black Lives Matter, black skin was not considered beautiful, not even in our own community. Conversation about bleaching cream was common.

When I was coming up as a young man, light-skinned African Americans were said to be "high yellow," or just "yellow." Among African Americans, folks who were yellow or who had "good hair" were considered more attractive than those of us who were darker skinned, had kinky hair, or facial features that were more associated with being African. Peppercorn Buddha hair like mine was the least desirable.

There is an old saying that I am embarrassed to recall: "If you're black, get back. If you're brown, stick around. If you're yellow, then you're mellow. And if you're white, you're all right." I heard this message for the first two decades of my life, and I am sorry to say that my experiences made me believe it.

To be honest, there were times when I hated myself, not because of anything I had done, but simply because of who I was. Even worse, because of this I thought there were things

I could never be. I had such a colossal inferiority complex. I remember hearing my elders ask, "What would white people think of you if they saw you doing that?" The entire moral standard received from Sunday school, vacation Bible school, and church worship services was to be as perfect a kid as possible, thinking that would win acceptance.

Every morning I would walk down the sidewalk to school and meet other students, coming from different parts of the neighborhood. We would walk together, all black kids. Sometimes the conversations would turn ugly and the older kids would be cruel, playing mean little tricks.

One kid would walk on one side of me and one kid on the other. When I was not looking, the other one would touch me on the shoulder, and I would not know who did it. Sometimes a boy behind me would slap me upside the head. In the 1950s your hair was extremely short if you were a boy. I was young and my bald head was an attraction for abuse by the bullies. They treated me like a punching bag.

One day I became tired of it and I reacted with profanity. The minute I said those terrible words, everybody froze. "We thought you were a Christian," they said. I dropped my head. I felt terrible. I was so ashamed. I had been tested and I had failed.

The next day, when I came out of my house, I walked down the steps past our little front lawn on my left to the sidewalk. I stopped and looked down the block to my left. I thought about how I had been humiliated and how I had violated my baptism by using profanity. For the rest of my junior and senior high school career, I would no longer turn left on the sidewalk in front of our home, but I would go right to West Broad Street, taking a different route to school.

Broad Street was not an average thoroughfare. It divided Columbus in half, north from south. It was Route 40, which started at Atlantic City, New Jersey, and ended at San Francisco, California, the route the early pioneers took west seeking a better life. It was the highway taken by Abraham Lincoln's funeral procession from Washington, D.C., to Springfield, Illinois. Not only did I take a different path, I made the decision from that day forward to walk alone. And I did. I remember saying to myself that I would not really be alone, because on Broad Street, all the way from Oakley Avenue to Powell Avenue, I could see car and truck license plates from all around the world. I also had cosmic companionship because, as my pastor, Jacob Julian Ashburn said on Sundays, God was omnipresent. That meant that Jesus would be with me. I would not be walking alone. Jesus would be at my side. I started to believe in eternal omnipresence.

From the eighth grade to the twelfth grade, early morning and late afternoon, in the rain, sunshine, and snow, I would sing hymns and walk to school, and I would return the same way. I literally separated myself to avoid the violence that those bullies had provoked in me. I enjoyed my peaceful solitary walk down a historic street communing with all the human traffic of the world and dreaming of places I would someday visit. West Broad Street and West High School, indeed, led me from the Occident to the Orient.

One of my favorite songs, which I still hum softly sometimes, was taught to me by my pastor's wife, Helen B. Ashburn.
For more than fifty years, I have been singing it over and
over again. It's been my chant, my Nam-myoho-renge-kyo:

We shall walk through the valley in peace.
We shall walk through the valley in peace.
If Jesus himself shall be our leader,
we shall walk through the valley in peace.

We shall meet our brother there.
We shall meet our sister there.
If Jesus himself shall be our leader,
we shall walk through the valley in peace.

Hence, it was not surprising, in light of my love for this song,
when Pastor Ashburn chose me to compete in the Central
Ohio Prince of Peace Speech Contest. We were asked to
commit to memory one speech on peace provided by the
contest host. I won the first contest in the black community
and lost the second contest in the white community. But
this 1958 speech launched my career speaking about peace
around the world.

Chapter Three

Meeting My Mentor

Nonviolence is not simply the absence of physical violence. Nonviolence, or ahimsa as it is called in Gandhian terms, is based on a commitment to honor the humanity and respect the dignity of others—in thought, in word, and in deed, even when we disagree with people, perhaps especially then. As a movement, nonviolent social change is an assertive, organized emergence of goodwill. Nonviolent social change is not easy. It is not quick. And it cannot be accomplished by the faint of heart.

My understanding of nonviolence, the ways that it shaped my education and, ultimately, my life were all set in motion by "the sound and the fury" of Martin Luther King Jr.

I first met him when I was in high school.

I was going to Sunday school one morning, and as I headed up the steps in front of the church, the superintendent of the Sunday school, Joseph Gentry, stopped me. He announced, "You're going with me this morning."

I was surprised. "Where are we going?" I asked. He was suggesting I was not going to Sunday school, which was highly irregular.

"You are going with me. We are going across town to hear Martin Luther King Jr."

Oh no, was my first thought. "My mother does not know about this."

"I have already called her," he assured me.

I was stunned. That was unprecedented. I did not even know he knew my mother.

"She approves of you going," he told me, and I was in such a state of shock I never thought to ask him why.

King had already begun to make a name for himself, especially in the African American community, but I can honestly say that I did not have the slightest inkling of the effect he was going to have on our nation, the world, or me.

We went to Union Grove Baptist Church, pastored by Morehouse College alumnus Phale D. Hale, to hear King preach. Unfortunately, I do not remember a word of King's sermon. I was considering the idea of becoming a minister at that time, so I consistently asked pastors if I could see their office libraries, their studies. Pastor Hale said: "Go right in. Nobody's in there."

I walked alone into Hale's study and closed the door. There were books from floor to ceiling, and I was excited but very quiet. I loved looking at books, and I loved seeing the libraries that pastors kept. I remember thinking that Hale's was magnificent.

Books were a refuge from a harsh and difficult world when I was a boy, and I came to love reading and exploring great ideas. My love of reading grew out of the solace, the secrets, and wisdom that reading gave me. These books allowed me to vicariously travel the world without leaving home.

I had started to look through the shelves when I felt someone's eyes on me, someone watching me intently. I turned to find someone sitting in a chair in the corner of the room. To my surprise it was Martin Luther King Jr. sitting there in the library, all alone.

I was speechless, but I remember my first thought: "Hale didn't tell me the truth. There is someone here!" I felt awkward. This was a setup, I realized. What I didn't know was that the universe was setting me up.

Knowing Morehouse men, I knew Hale was looking at me as a candidate. Because that is what Morehouse men do: recruit other men to Morehouse.

King looked at me for another moment, smiled, and then broke the silence. "What is your name?"

I introduced myself. I felt a little nervous, like I had been caught someplace I was not supposed to be, so I explained that Dr. Hale had given me permission to look at his library. I told King that the reason I was looking was because I was thinking of becoming a minister someday.

King appeared interested and asked me seriously, "Have you considered college?"

I told him I had, named some of the ones I was considering but admitted that I did not know which one would best prepare me for ministry.

King nodded and asked, "Have you considered Morehouse?"

Morehouse, of course, was King's alma mater, and I knew this at the time. But despite that, I just said the next thing that came into my head.

"I thought about it, but my neighbor said it is not up to snuff." In those days, the historically black colleges were often considered inferior to white schools, even among many African Americans.

Well, King was certainly surprised to hear me say this! He did not speak for a moment, but once he gathered his thoughts, he became animated and forceful in his recommendation of Morehouse.

"I beg to differ," King began. "Morehouse College is an outstanding school." Then he spent some time recruiting me to the Atlanta institution.

I decided that very day that, yes, I wanted to study at Morehouse, and my desire to learn reached a fever pitch.

My high school had a reputation for sending many of its graduates to college, but the teachers were all white and my grades were mediocre. But I was determined. There was one English teacher, in particular, Adolph Kittel, who had a great reputation. Besides which, he drove the latest Lincoln Continental, a car I admired and imagined I would own someday.

I remember the day I approached him.

He was standing, immaculately dressed, in the doorway

of his classroom. He seemed a nice gentleman and I really admired him. I had tacitly chosen him as someone to emulate. "I'd like you to teach me how to write," I told him.

He just shook his head. "Larry, I don't know how to teach you how to write."

That response totally confused me, because he was an English teacher with huge classes. Of course he could teach me how to write! But nothing I could say would make him interested in doing so. There was a gap between us in his mind, and it seemed to be race related. He had taught at West High School for twenty-four years by the time I started my senior year in 1959. He was a graduate of Capital University and The Ohio State University. He consented to autograph his picture in my yearbook. But I concluded that he just did not like people like me, which saddened me. I knew it was racism. But I made a decision that I was going to excel at this school anyway and win some distinct honor. I became more determined on that day to be the class speaker at my graduation and to give a speech worthy of Dr. King.

I started working on a speech in the tenth grade that I hoped would be good enough for me to successfully compete to be senior class speaker. I knew I needed help, so I asked my neighbor, a retired schoolteacher, Rosa Carter Triggs, to instruct me; she was also an active member of my church, the Oakley Baptist Church. She proofread everything I wrote and worked with me until the tryouts in the second semester of my senior year. There were five of us auditioning to be graduation speaker, and I was the only

African American. My speech was titled "The Hand That Rocks the Cradle Rules the World."

I delivered my speech to the faculty committee, including Edwin M. Kaylor, the chairman. He was also my career guidance counselor and a speech teacher. When the final decision was announced, I'd come in second, which meant that I would not be speaking at graduation. I knew the speech that won was not superior to mine, but I did not feel a grudge. I knew I had done something really fine. But an interesting thing happened the following year.

I went off to a college in Virginia that my church leadership had chosen for me, against my mother's wishes. When I returned to visit my high school a year later, I saw Kaylor.

We were walking down the corridor together when he asked me how I was doing. I told him I was doing rather well. "I do have a question though," I added. "I was really surprised that I did not win the speech contest."

"That is very interesting," he answered. "Because your speech was the best."

I was stunned. "It was? Then why is it that I did not win?"

"You know I was chairman of the committee. But that also meant that I did not have a vote. You will recall that your twelfth grade English composition teacher, Mrs. Jane A. Thomas, was on that committee, and after you left the room, she told the committee that she did not think you could write that well."

"I wrote it," I responded. I told him how I had started working on the speech in the tenth grade. But I did not ask him why the committee had not invited me back into the room to ask me how I had produced such a good speech.

Still, West High was known for bringing many outstanding personalities for the student body to hear, people who broadened our horizons and our thinking as global citizens. We heard from the famous advice columnist pen-named Ann Landers (Esther Pauline Lederer) to Thomas Anthony Dooley III, a famous gay Roman Catholic physician who fundraised globally for hospitals in refugee camps of Vietnam and Laos, to E. Stanley Jones, a missionary and theologian who spent much time with Gandhi and Nehru and electrified our student body with his oratory.

I will never forget the day when all classes were interrupted by our principal, Robert F. Darrow, with an announcement over the public address system that all classes were to assemble in the great West High auditorium. The Yale University Choir, passing through Columbus on buses headed for Connecticut, had been intercepted by the superintendent of schools, Harold Eibling. The choir director had consented to give a spontaneous concert for West High School students. By the time all twenty-three hundred of us rushed to our seats, the big red curtain of the stage opened and the massive Yale Choir was standing, attired immaculately, in full view. The sight was breathtaking, and next came the Columbus Symphony Orchestra.

One of the best speakers I have ever heard was Kaylor's pastor, Otis A. Maxfield, a graduate in pastoral psychology and counseling from Boston University. All of the students who were interested in the ministry met Maxfield after his Career Day assembly speech. I was invited not only to his church but to his Camp Akita in southern Ohio, and we began a lifelong friendship.

All of this majority cultural exposure helped to expand my awareness of the world and paved the way for my receptivity to Japanese Nichiren Buddhist spirituality. But white culture did not always understand how it presented itself to members of minority communities. It was not always clear to white people why racial minorities felt excluded. People who are oppressed feel the signs of racism miles away. In academia, racism often shows up as low expectations. My mother was right when she told me, "You have to be able to drive your car and your neighbor's too in order to avoid a wreck." Or, as the "last great school master," Benjamin E. Mays, put it, "He who starts behind in the great race of life must forever remain behind or run faster than the man in front."[11] Like many other young black people, I was not happy about this. But I was proud that I was, in fact, able to "run twice as fast" and succeed in what I set out to do. And I am aware, too, that I had the support of good teachers and friends, many white, who believed in me and understood how to encourage me.

But no one encouraged me more than Martin Luther King Jr. himself. During my freshman year at Virginia Seminary and College (currently Virginia University of Lynchburg), I heard him speak again. It was March 12, 1961, and his speech was titled "The American Dream." It was one of two speeches King gave during his People-to-People Tour to introduce himself to the nation.

In a single evening, his voice lifted me and more than four thousand other students and citizens of Lynchburg at the E.C. Glass High School auditorium out of our seats no less than four times. You could not keep your seat. He drew us to our feet with the most powerful oratory I had heard before or since. Even then, we did not know what to do with the new energy King's words ignited in us. People rose up, their arms went up. My arms went up. When our arms were as high as they could stretch, we screamed, "Yesssss!" to the heavens. King's voice tapped into something so visceral within each of us that we had to respond orally, dramatically, and physically. We were experiencing the *mysterium tremendum*, that is, the most profound of spiritual experiences, at once fascinating, terrifying, and totally arresting. The pounding waterfall of eloquent, magisterial, and poetic words that were the sound of King's baritone voice fell upon my ears like the thunderous affirmation of God, and I knew I would never be the same. My life had been changed forever.

He spoke of the vision of equality that had founded our nation. He spoke of the equality of the races. He spoke of why the fight for freedom must be nonviolent and what that meant. He spoke of the power of the ballot and the need to register and vote. And, even then, he spoke of the beloved community, the neighborhood of the world, and the need for all men to see one another as brothers and sisters. There was a clear message that the humanity and value of people do indeed transcend the sovereignty of nations, the unscientific concept of race, and the discriminatory laws of the state.

"The American Dream will not become a reality devoid of the larger dream of a world of brotherhood, of peace, and goodwill. The world in which we live is a world of geographical oneness and we are challenged now to make it spiritually one."[12]

We rose to our feet and our hearts sang.

"The great problem confronting us today is that we have allowed the means by which we live to outdistance the ends for which we live. We have allowed our civilization to outrun our culture, and so we are in danger now of ending up with guided missiles in the hands of misguided men."[13]

We clapped, we cheered. Again, we were on our feet.

"We must make full and constructive use of the freedom we already possess. We must not use our oppression as an excuse for mediocrity and laziness. For history has proven that inner determination can often break through the outer shackles of circumstance."[14]

"Yes," I shouted. This was what I believed. This was what I was trying to do. I was so inspired, I knew I would never think the same way about myself or the world. I would literally divide my life into before that speech and after that speech.

"I believe more than ever before in the power of nonviolent resistance. It has a moral aspect tied to it. It makes it possible for the individual to secure moral ends through moral means."[15]

King's life was a testament to everything in which he spoke. He averaged five speeches per day and slept an average of four hours per night. We know this in part because he was betrayed by one of his staff members who took money to inform the FBI of his schedule. King was hounded by J. Edgar Hoover, who bugged his telephone and hotel rooms, circulated salacious gossip about him, and even tried to force him into committing suicide after he received the Nobel Peace Prize. King was the first person to be prosecuted by the state of Alabama on two counts of perjury on his state income tax return, and still he managed to win the case.

While addressing an audience in Birmingham, a man mounted the stage and suddenly punched King in the face, while a shocked audience watched in amazement as King made no move to strike back or turn away. Instead, he looked at his assailant and spoke calmly to him. Within seconds, several people pulled the attacker away. While others led the crowd in song, King and his colleagues spoke with the assailant at the rear of the stage. Then King returned to the podium to tell the audience that the man was twenty-four-year-old Roy James, a member of the Nazi Party from Arlington, Virginia. King refused to press charges.

In DeKalb County, Georgia, King was guarded by a large German shepherd before he was sent to Reidsville Prison with handcuffs on his wrists and leg irons on his ankles. He was so lonely in this meanest of all prisons in the south that he later confessed to his wife that he had broken down and cried. Whites called him "Martin Luther Coon," and other black leaders called him "Martin Loser King."

Martin Luther King Jr. was jailed in Birmingham, Albany, Atlanta, Reidsville, Decatur, St. Augustine, and Selma. From 1955 to 1968, as he traveled around the nation, King refused to accept protection from police or the FBI. During one arrest, he was choked, kicked, tried, convicted, fined, jailed, spit upon, and cursed by a Montgomery police officer who also tried to break his arm. He never pressed charges.

Two powerful bombs exploded under and outside his hotel room in Birmingham. His house was bombed in Montgomery, with his wife and baby daughter inside. He was stabbed in New York City. He was stoned in Chicago, beaten in Selma, and booed in Los Angeles. They threw eggs at him in Harlem and heckled him in London. Racists threw a knife and stones at him in Cicero, Illinois. He received scores of life-threatening telephone calls and hate mail. By the time of his assassination in Memphis, he had gone through arrests, jail transfers, court hearings, and release proceedings twenty-nine times.

King's response to his suffering and trials was not "compassionate conservatism." It was extravagant love, unconditional charity, and responsibility. It was agape—the love which knows no boundaries. It has justice at its heart.

To this day, King remains the most powerful and electrifying speaker I have ever heard. It's hard to explain, but when I listened to him, I got a strong sense of what was possible for me to achieve. I saw in him the kind of man—smart, inspirational, intellectual, dedicated, exemplar, and black—I wanted to believe I could be.

So powerful was the effect of King's presence upon me that when he finished speaking I ran out of the auditorium back to the campus and telephoned my mother begging her to let me transfer to Morehouse College. I wanted to go where King had gone to college. I remembered him trying to recruit me in Pastor Hale's library at Union Grove Baptist Church. Foolishly, I had allowed a neighbor to talk me out of it. But that night my mother had her eye trained on the four jobs she had to work to keep me in college, and when I said "Morehouse," all she heard was more expense, more cost, more dollars that she did not have. I was too naive and self-absorbed to realize we could not afford it. She simply said no, something she had never said to my aspirations before. I hung up the phone, devastated.

But I lost neither my will nor my sense of reason. I sat there a moment and then, compelled by the power of King's words, quickly resolved that if I could not attend Morehouse College, I would do the second best thing—secure the remainder of my education at Boston University, where King attended graduate school. Surely I would receive the same excellent tutelage as King received during his PhD studies there and follow in his giant footsteps.

In my junior year, I borrowed money from my psychology professor, C.M. Cofield, and took the Greyhound bus to Boston. I was hosted by another college professor who had moved to Boston from Lynchburg, Virgil A. Wood. I went to classes, to chapel, and talked with professors. I met with Walter G. Muelder, the dean, who was most persuasive. He was an ecumenist and world-renowned social ethicist whose writing had greatly influenced King's evaluation of Reinhold Niebuhr's "conception of man." He told me that Boston University had a long history of admitting blacks and that they had graduated the largest number of African Americans with doctorates; but the year before, uncharacteristically, no blacks had been admitted to the School of Theology. With a copy of the New Testament in Greek in his hand, he told me that Boston University's School of Theology was the right place for me to prepare for a learned ministry.

I applied in my junior year of college and was immediately accepted. It was unheard of to be admitted to graduate school in your junior year. When the news spread in Lynchburg, I was a citywide celebrity, and everybody wanted to help me. Elsie Cofield spent many hours privately tutoring me in reading and comprehension. I received a tremendous send-off by my college pastor at the Court Street Baptist Church where Harold A. Carter Sr. invited me to deliver a farewell sermon, after I had served for three years as his pulpit assistant. Carter had been the pulpit assistant to Martin Luther King Jr. at the

Dexter Avenue Baptist Church in Montgomery while in college at Alabama State University. It was the best decision I ever made in my life to attend Boston University. Today, Walter Muelder's photograph hangs in the King Chapel library at Morehouse College and my second book is dedicated to him.

During my first year at Boston University, in winter 1964, King came to preach at Harvard's Memorial Church and I went to hear him.

Memorial Church was packed, but even though we were waiting for more than two hours, not a single person left. The president of Harvard, Nathan Marsh Pusey, was pacing the floor in front of the congregation anxiously. King was two hours late, having been delayed at Boston's Logan International Airport by the press who were eager to hear of the progress of the Civil Rights Movement.

There were overflow congregations around Harvard Yard in three campus locations. When King finally arrived, he gave his powerful "A Knock at Midnight" sermon:

> It is midnight within the social order. On the international horizon nations are engaged in a colossal and bitter contest for supremacy. Two world wars have been fought within a generation, and the clouds of another war are dangerously low. Man now has atomic and nuclear weapons that could within seconds completely destroy the major cities of the world. Yet the arms race continues and nuclear tests still explode in

the atmosphere, with the grim prospect that the very air we breathe will be poisoned by radioactive fallout. Will these circumstances and weapons bring the annihilation of the human race?[16]

Everyone listened raptly.

Afterward, I lined up in the center aisle to greet King on the chancel steps. When I got to him, I asked: "Do you remember me? We met at Dr. Hale's church in Columbus, Ohio, and you recruited me to Morehouse. I'm at Boston University now."

He smiled and said that, yes, he remembered me. I had not thought to bring any of his books for him to sign, so I asked him to sign the book I had in my hand. I had an assignment in my religion and personality course, so I had the text for that class, *Lives in Progress*.

He seemed a little surprised and spent a moment looking at the cover, but he opened it up and signed it anyway. I did not think much about it at the time, but when I think back on it now, I'm embarrassed that I asked him to sign someone else's book! The truth is I was so focused on keeping up with my course reading that I did not dare part from my required textbooks for even a moment.

I met King one other time when he was in Boston to speak at the Ford Hall Forum of the New England Conservatory of Music. We spoke casually for about ten minutes on the street after his speech. I do not remember that conversation. It was so amazing to be standing on the sidewalk, talking casually with Martin Luther King Jr. He was just a regular person—down to earth, unassuming, unpretentious, a humble human being. I did not know it, but that would be the last time I would ever see him face to face.

King came to Boston once more for a peace march. I was looking forward to joining it. Not only was the Civil Rights Movement that he was spearheading of great personal meaning to me, but I also loved the atmosphere of such events. I had been very active in the nonviolent resistance movement during my undergraduate studies at Virginia Seminary and College. There was a feeling of pride, of empowerment, and of positive energy at these events, and they gave me the drive and focus to pursue my personal dreams and goals. But, of course, I mostly wanted to attend this particular rally because I would have the opportunity to hear King speak again.

But when the time came to go join the march, I was buried in my schoolwork. Though it was a hard decision, I resolved to stay in my dorm room and study. In retrospect, this was a foolish choice. But you have to understand what I was feeling at the time. I felt my classmates were progressing easily through their work and would leave me behind if I did not work extra hard. Not only should I have had more belief in my ability to do good work in school— even more, if I had known that this time in Boston might be my last opportunity to see King, I would have made a different decision.

I never imagined that King's life might be cut short. I believed that my life and his would have many more occasions to intersect—and when I did see him, I wanted to be able to tell him that I was doing well in my PhD program at Boston University. In a way, my decision not to go to his march was motivated by my desire to become the kind of person I felt he would want me to be.

As a young man, I set out with a deep desire to become a doctor of the church in the image of Martin Luther King Jr. This was the desire that King and Otis Maxfield together created within me, to strive always to balance the tension between righteous reflection and faithful action. King caused me to devote my life to transformation on a personal, social, and moral global scale, and Maxfield caused me to obtain my doctorate in his field of pastoral psychology and counseling. Having this expertise, then I could deliver sermons as counseling to address individual and social concerns, demonstrating the steps to being the change itself. King caused me to stand for justice, peace, and to love my enemies. Maxfield caused me to want to change myself and to change the world. From 1958 to 1968, I read every sermon that Maxfield preached, and years later, when I was dean at Morehouse, I would nominate him to succeed William Sloan Coffin as senior minister at Riverside Church in New York City.

For some time, I knew that Martin Luther King Jr. would be my lifelong mentor and moral cosmopolitan exemplar for interpreting what global socialized Christian spirituality looks, feels, acts, and sounds like. I vowed always to be his disciple in whatever way Spirit directed, in whatever way it would lead me, and to do something significant for him before I closed my eyes for the final time.

Chapter Four

Turning Poison Into Medicine

The idea of a mentor is common in Asia. Many Eastern spiritual traditions refer to the lineage of their descent, and this lineage can be traced from disciple to teacher back to an ancient source. Whether they refer to that mentor as a teacher, a master, or a guru, this idea is fundamental to the Eastern understanding of the transmission and development of spiritual thought.

Many of us have heard the Japanese word *sensei*, or "teacher." Students in Japanese grade schools commonly refer to their teachers as *sensei*. But the word can also suggest a relationship that runs much deeper and is far more important in an individual's life than a person responsible for classroom instruction.

The word is also used to address a master of a certain craft or skill. As in the old European guild systems, where a master craftsman would accept someone as an apprentice to learn a trade, a *sensei* is someone who has mastered a trade or craft, or even a way of being, and we dedicate ourselves to this person to learn from them. In Japan, many traditional arts, such as calligraphy or *ikebana* flower arranging, are taught by *senseis* to generations of students. In the West, we are probably most familiar with the word in its martial arts context, where a *sensei* will teach students judo or karate.

Because the master is respected, people trust the apprentice and, conversely, people come to hold the master in higher esteem when his or her disciples achieve great accomplishments.

Asian spiritual communities often place great significance on their lineage, the line of teachings formed by teachers transmitting their thought and practice, their enlightened understanding, to a group of disciples, one or more of whom will become teachers in their own right to a new generation. This idea of lineage is also central to how one understands doctrine, practice, and ritual among the various spiritual traditions. Entire schools of thought and religious communities have been formed by lineage-based communities.

From this perspective, choosing a mentor is a crucial decision for any serious spiritual seeker. This decision defines the spiritual tradition with which a person identifies and the worldview within which that person will strive to make their mark on posterity.

This idea of fidelity to a *sensei* and practice within a community defined by lineage stands in contrast to what I see as the spiritual fashion of America today. Here, many people view spiritual growth as a purely individual endeavor, where one can choose an idea from this tradition, a ritual from that one, to fashion a wholly individual, even idiosyncratic, spiritual worldview. While spiritual growth is certainly personal and intimate, I do not know that the path a person walks is so entirely individual. It might be the case that making the effort to practice within a community of believers, and to understand a particular school of thought, has much to offer the genuine seeker of spirituality, something that is lost from a more casual pick-and-choose approach to spiritual learning. In the understanding of the theologian Dietrich Bonhoeffer, becoming a disciple includes a sense of duty and a set of obligations. Discipleship, in other words, is not necessarily easy. It comes at a cost. Specifically, Bonhoeffer says that grace—the unconditional and unearned love of God—has a cost. He "called people to the costly grace of following Jesus and obeying his commands. He put his theological perspective into this sentence: 'Only the one who obeys believes, and only the one who believes obeys.' . . . Faith and obedience can never be separated."[17] Bonhoeffer was a committed theologian in action, constantly rethinking the meaning of serving God, loving neighbors, and, always, telling the truth. He was a teacher, a moralist, a resistance fighter, a prisoner, and ultimately a martyr.

This is an understanding of discipleship that I share. I am called to be a disciple of Jesus, and to answer that call requires effort on my part—and living up to the self-acknowledged ideals of discipleship as obligatory and imperative. I do not regard the language Bonhoeffer chooses to use of "submitting" to the "yoke" of Jesus as particularly onerous or off putting because I find joy in freely choosing this sort of submission. For me, there is a great deal of individual freedom in my personal decision to accept Jesus as the model of what humanity can be.

Being a disciple is not the same as joining a club. It is not as simple as declaring allegiance or choosing a side. It is a purposeful decision to try to understand the greater vision held by a mentor and to try to actualize that vision in our own life. The decision to be a disciple is fundamentally a choice about the values, virtues, and vision of victory we have for ourselves and the world, and how to avoid vices.

For me, the visionary mentor who shaped my life was Martin King, the voice and architect of our American nonviolent Civil Rights Movement. King's leadership of this movement lasted for just over a decade, but in that time, the movement he spearheaded spread from the buses of Montgomery to the halls of Congress. He sparked sweeping changes in America. The work he began goes on today and continues to shape and push the world toward greater respect for one another, ethical pluralism for international engagement, and toward extending equal rights, equal opportunities, and human dignity to all people. My admiration for King knows no bounds. Meeting him personally had a profound impact on my life, and his death—and the promise I made at that time—have determined the direction that my life has taken since the evening of April 4, 1968.

Persons my age remember what life was like before the Civil Rights Movement. I am of a generation of African Americans who holds Martin King with reverence. We heard a man speak an eloquent and mighty truth to power and to speak from ultimate power the truth. We felt the moral veracity of what he said. Many of us were inspired and empowered by King's courage in standing up to entrenched political, social, and religious institutions of power. I do not know that we had ever felt these things before with such intensity and galvanizing strength. For the first time we believed that we might know in our lifetimes the truth of the phrase from the Gospels of Mark and Luke that the last shall be first.[18] King helped me find my prophetic, moral, cosmopolitan voice.

By 1968 I was seriously involved with the woman who would become my wife, Marva Lois Griffin. One spring night we were out on a date witnessing a play at Boston University about the assassination of Abraham Lincoln. I will never forget it. The details are as clear to me today as if they happened last night.

At the intermission Marva and I remained seated in the small theater of Boston University's George Sherman Student Union. Suddenly, I noticed that the venerable dean of the School of Theology, Walter George Muelder, stepped into the theater, tapped on the shoulder my homiletics professor, Robert Luccock, seated directly in front of me. Muelder beckoned him to come out of the theater onto the second floor plaza. Initially, I did not think anything of this observation, as I continued to talk with Marva about the actors in the play being directed by a classmate in the School of Theology. Intermittently, I took sidelong glances over my left shoulder at the two tall men facing each other engaged in what seemed a very troubling and sober conversation. I had not seen such expressions on their faces before. I had a terrible feeling that something was wrong, so I excused myself and walked across the aisle and stepped up onto the plaza to Muelder. I asked, "Is something wrong?" I had no idea that I was about to hear news that would change my life so decisively.

He turned to me as I approached and looked stricken.

"Martin Luther King Jr. was shot this evening."

I recoiled in shock. The news felt like a knife stabbing me in the heart. I did not know what to think; in fact, I could not think at all. I felt like I was about to lose consciousness. There was no sound. I stopped breathing for a few seconds. The entire world came to a stop, as my heart sunk.

I was struggling, swimming in an ocean of fear. I slowly lifted my head and asked, "Is he all right?" I did not want to consider the worst.

Muelder's eyes filled with sadness. In the quietest of voices he answered, "Thirty minutes ago, he died."

I thought I might collapse.

I don't remember the next few minutes very well. Somehow I made my way back to Marva, and without a word, I took her by the hand. Together, we walked away from the theater and down the great staircase into the Commonwealth Avenue lobby of the student union and onto the wide sidewalk of one of Boston's busiest streets. It was literally a dark evening. The automobiles with bright headlights were moving in both directions at normal speeds, seemingly indifferent to the news that I thought should have stopped everything.

Marva must have asked me what was wrong and I must have told her. But I only remember our silence as we walked east down Commonwealth Avenue, holding hands as tightly as we could, without any hope of consolation. We soon found ourselves in front of Daniel L. Marsh Chapel at the heart of the university. At that hour, the modern Gothic building was unlit. Neither one of us had consciously decided to go there, but I suppose it was only natural to be somewhere, anywhere, sacred in this never-to-be-forgotten moment.

We walked up the granite stairs through the narthex into the sanctuary and sat on the last pew in the dark, to the left of the center aisle. Above us on the distant wall was a majestic stained glass image of Christ, and beneath him, in the shadows, were the carved wooden statues of the four doctors of the Church: Matthew, Mark, Luke, and John. In a higher place, the lights of the city illuminated the beautiful stained glass window of Christ in judgement to the nations in the last days.

Tears were streaming down our faces. From somewhere deep within, the words welled up. I prayed aloud, "Lord, help me to do something significant for Martin Luther King Jr. before I close my eyes."

Then and there I decided that I would spend the rest of my life furthering the work of King. Before I had felt the inspiration of mentorship, now I felt the responsibility and the obligation of the mentee.

I was sorrowful that we would never hear his voice again address the pressing issues of our time from the ethical edge of his most relevant cosmopolitan theological perspective. But I was also young, with my life ahead of me, and I knew that I had work to do. Men might kill the body of Martin Luther King Jr., but his legacy could not be destroyed. The message of his work would not be lost—not if I had anything to do with it.

I knew what it was to lose a beloved mentor, a leader, a teacher, and a role model. I knew how easy it was to give into that loss, to wallow in sadness or despair, anger, rage, or bitterness. But I also now knew what it was to make a different decision regarding how to respond to that grief, especially since I had been very naive about the nature of evil in the world. In that moment, I chose to live with my eyes fixed firmly on the north star of King's highest aspirations, building the beloved world community, and I already knew that following that invitation by fire would take me to marvelous places.

As a Christian minister, to be a disciple was first and foremost to be a disciple of Jesus, practicing the religion of Jesus. Jesus said, "I am not come to destroy, but to fulfil."[19]

He was saying, in effect, that "I have come to practice, to be the thing itself, to be the change I wish to see." This was why he was the Word made flesh.

When a person responds to the call to be a disciple, something is fulfilled. We are realizing something more than duty, something more like the truest part of who we are. In my faith, I regard discipleship as the Word being made flesh, as the teachings find the Spirit of breath and life in the world. Jesus did not teach us simply to aspire to heaven in the afterlife, to be futurist. He called us to practice and anchor his teachings in this world today. You will have heaven because you have made a decision to be heaven on earth, today. "Today you'll be with me in paradise,"[20] Jesus says.

So many years later, when I began to learn about the Soka Gakkai, I would discover what that movement's second president, Josei Toda, said when he learned that his own mentor, Tsunesaburo Makiguchi, had died in a Japanese prison. He, too, vowed to accomplish something great to repay his mentor. He, too, wanted to show the world his mentor through what he would do.

I had been called as a disciple of Jesus to contribute something to continuing the legacy of Martin Luther King Jr. I will never forget that terrible night when I learned that he was dead. But it was also on that night that I decided I would do whatever was in my power to make sure that his life and legacy were not forgotten. This was a promise I made in my heart. I was lost in grief, rage, and tears, but I made a decision that night that, while evil people might kill the prince of peace, I would make sure that his ideas would survive. I realize now that this was not just a vow I made; it was, in fact, my calling and my vocation.

It is important to think about what it means to turn away from bitterness, especially after severe and painful circumstances. We have to understand the temptation to give way to anger, because from this temptation comes the impulse to demonize, to blame others for what we encountered, and to become mean-spirited.

The Buddhists say that everybody chooses their time to be born. If that is true, then I probably did not choose an earlier time because I would have been another Nat Turner. There is something in me that is for the underdog. I hate injustice. And because of that, I am capable of tremendous rage. My mother used to say to me as a kid: "I am not letting you go down south this summer, because I will have to come down there and kill somebody. Your mouth is too big. I am gonna keep you up here in Columbus, Ohio."

As a young African American man born in the American South before the Civil Rights Movement, I understand the temptation to harbor hatred against the segregationists and terrorists. Though I left Georgia at the age of five, I have experienced racism and exclusion firsthand. I have felt anger, even rage, about the legalized oppression of African Americans and state-sponsored terrorism. I also understand the temptation to be distrustful or hateful of all white people and to envy those who have more material wealth. But I made a conscious decision to turn from these bitter thoughts because of family and church school teachings. As a result, my anger did not define or consume me. I learned to see, and to name, the evil in the world without feeling victimized by others.

Even so, in 1968, when a white assassin's bullet ended King's life, my heart was torn asunder with anger and hatred for whites everywhere, no matter who they were, because I felt they had not done enough to help him. My hatred was blind and indiscriminate. All the while, I knew that my mentor would have been ashamed of me and my bitter heart. Indeed, for one year, even as a disciple of King's nonviolent philosophy, I fell short. Until, at last, I prayed prayers strong enough to change my destiny, prayers mighty enough to pry my heart free from the rage that had seized me.

When I met Daisaku Ikeda, I learned that in his Buddhist worldview this kind of praying was referred to as "changing poison into medicine." Buddhists use what is difficult or painful in their lives as a source of growth.

Ikeda himself knew what it was to turn away from anger toward compassion, and to use pain as the fuel to create a better world. After World War II, he could have been angry at the Japanese government for the destruction of his family home, the loss of his childhood, the death of his brother, and the difficulties he faced in pursuing his education in that war-ravaged country. He could have become bitter toward the Americans for their use of nuclear bombs in Hiroshima and Nagasaki on August 6 and 9, 1945, or suspicious of the occupying forces throughout Japan. Instead, this became fuel for Ikeda's passionate commitment to peace and his profound and lifelong dedication to fostering a type of education that encourages creativity in the young and gives them tools to build lives of happiness and value.

King was a source of personal inspiration to me since I was a young man, and he continues to inspire generations of young people from all ethnic stripes in the decades since his assassination. Sometimes, however, when we make someone a hero, as we have done with King, we honor their life but keep them distant from the living. We no longer have to be responsible for embodying their teachings. We free ourselves from the duties and obligations of discipleship.

This is my lineage. But a "calling" is not just a way of making a living. It's about making a life. It's about living a life shaped by the vision of another, dedicated to a path first walked by our mentor. It is about finding what it is that gives meaning to one's life.

Chapter Five

Morehouse Mission

I have been blessed in my calling to be able to return to my beautiful native Georgia, which I never wanted to leave. It was a real answer to my prayers that when I did return, legal segregation had come to an end. Raising a healthy family in Georgia seemed a greater possibility. In 1979 I was offered a position as assistant professor of religion at Morehouse College, a historically black male institution, Martin Luther King Jr.'s alma mater. In addition, I was appointed the first dean of the Martin Luther King Jr. Memorial Chapel, beginning July 1. At last, I was going to fulfill my desire to go to Morehouse. King had recruited me as a tenth grader, and I was finally answering the call, while also returning to my birth state, which I left in 1946 at the age of five upon the death of my maternal grandmother, Willie Mae Mullins.

It is not possible to fully understand Martin Luther King Jr. unless his life is placed within the context of Morehouse College and its founder, who set the brand for the Augusta and Atlanta institution. King could not have graduated from another liberal arts college in the United

States and have been so inspired to achieve as he did because Morehouse personalities started the American nonviolent Civil Rights Movement.

Morehouse College was founded by William Jefferson White on Valentines Day, February 14, 1867, in the Silver Bluff Springfield Baptist Church, just two years after the Civil War ended and the African slaves were emancipated by President Abraham Lincoln. White was founder and pastor of Augusta's Harmony Baptist Church, the second home of the Augusta Institute, which would become Morehouse College in 1913.[21]

White was born in 1831. His father was white, but his mother was black with Native American heritage. Using the *Blue Black Speller*, and a little help from his mother, he taught himself to read as a young boy and decided to become a carpenter and minister. Even though he could pass for white, he worshipped as black and married black, and just after the Civil War in 1866 he organized the first equal rights association in Georgia in old Silver Bluff Springfield Baptist Church, founded in 1787. White was radically dedicated to championing legislation to level the playing field between the races.

In December 1905, White issued the call for the first Equal Rights Convention of black Georgians to be held in Macon, Georgia, and to consider a wide variety of grievances. There were five hundred delegates at that convention, one of whom was Martin Luther King Jr.'s maternal grandfather, A.D. Williams, an 1898 graduate of Atlanta Baptist College (the name of Morehouse College from 1897 to 1913).

Another delegate and organizer was Atlanta Baptist College president-elect John Hope, a mentee and former employee of White. Atlanta Baptist College alumnus Peter James Bryant, pastor of Atlanta's Wheat Street Baptist Church, was also present. Atlanta University professor W.E.B. Du Bois was in attendance and delivered the keynote address. White was elected to give the presidential address as the venerated patriarch of Georgia's Negro Baptists.[22]

From early on, 1850–65, White was conducting clandestine schools to teach Negroes to read in the homes of interracial couples in Augusta, which was against Georgia law at the time. He sought to cultivate independent and freethinking men, even at the risk of legal prosecution. General Oliver Otis Howard, a Civil War hero and Freedmen's Bureau commissioner, for whom Howard University is named, hired White to help institute Reconstruction for the newly freed Negroes. He located and cleared large plots of land for schools to be built across the South, becoming known as the Father of Public Education for Negroes in Augusta.

White also founded a newspaper, in 1882, the *Georgia Baptist*, and is said to have been the most influential black journalist of his day. W.E.B. DuBois said that with the reach of the *Georgia Baptist*, White held a hundred thousand Negroes in the palm of his hand. For that reason perhaps— being founded by a journalist—Morehouse College has always emphasized writing in every aspect of its curriculum. White understood the importance of the written word and the power of writing effectively as the prelude to being well spoken. He was a protégé of Frederick Douglass, who also used his newspaper, the *North Star*, to fight for equal rights for blacks. White was constantly on the run for his life because he was viewed as a threat to dismantling segregation's Jim Crow laws.

Originally, Morehouse College was called the Augusta Institute since it began with the elementary subjects for the uneducated newly freed slaves. There were other institutions established around the same time with the aim of educating African American men and women, in particular Tuskegee Institute, founded by Booker T. Washington. But Washington's vision emphasized industrial education. His credo was "self-reliance" because he believed that the African American community needed to develop skills in agriculture and other important trades in the rural South so they could achieve economic independence.

The leadership of Morehouse had a different idea. They felt that a strong liberal arts education was essential to raise a generation of men schooled in writing and versed in history, philosophy, and religion who would be able to engage in political and transcendent critiques of the social system and inspire the embodiment of the highest nobility, while preaching a liberating activist black social gospel. Essentially, it was their intention to foster a generation of Negro leaders able to remove the legal and philosophical hinge pin that held segregation on its doorpost.

The black Baptist prophetic justice tradition was at the heart of the school, but eventually the college's leadership felt that church control was too limiting. John Hope and W.E.B. DuBois among other leaders wanted the school to be more than a Bible college. Hope and the college trustees wanted this school to emphasize a liberal arts education, and in 1929 the Baptist control of Morehouse was terminated so that the school could develop the analytical skills of a new generation of nonviolent freedom fighters.

During this same period in history, halfway around the world, Tsunesaburo Makiguchi, the Soka Gakkai's first president, was championing a different philosophy of education from the prevailing schools of pedagogy dominant in Japan. He also sought to cultivate free and creative individuals rather than produce loyal subjects of the state, and for this he was persecuted and prosecuted by government authorities. His disciple, Josei Toda, was, like William Jefferson White, a publisher and author. Toda founded a newspaper, the *Seikyo Shimbun*, just as White had, because he believed in the power of the written word to influence society.

Morehouse was founded with the mission to educate African American men at a time when this was regarded as a fool's errand. It was a courageous action, one that reflected a belief in the value and potential of young black men that society at large did not share. Later, as the school evolved, it left its formal Baptist affiliation, not out of rejection but out of an awareness that the demands of the times required that the school grow beyond industrial education and religious fundamentalism. The college had to evolve in order to stay true to its radical belief in the potential of young African

American men as contributors to their communities able to change the world and true to the black social justice reading of the religion of Jesus.

Nevertheless, even today, students come to Morehouse having been referred by pastors. If I have religion and philosophy majors in my classes, I also have believers and seekers. Students call all times of the day and night—not just to my phone but to the phones of all their professors—and are treated as sons. Many students come to Morehouse because of this reputation and because one of the hallmarks of historically black colleges is to teach students who come out of weak high school backgrounds. But an essential part of that mission is a family-like nurturing environment. As a faculty, we are very accessible. And we are legendary for taking coal and turning it into diamonds!

When I first arrived at Morehouse, it was not unusual to hear students say, "I am the first person in my family to attend college." You do not hear that quite as much anymore, but every now and then there will be a student who lets me know in his junior year that he does not really live on campus. "I have been sleeping in my car," he will say to me. Or, "I have been sleeping on the floor of somebody else's room."

We had one young man who came to Morehouse and brought his daughter to school every day for four years. She went everywhere with him, even to the gym. When he graduated, the faculty and his entire class gave him a standing ovation as he crossed the stage. It was miraculous. The students have tremendous respect for this place with its high expectations and how it makes them feel, as it holds a crown over their heads with the hope that they will grow tall enough to wear it.

Martin King graduated from Morehouse with a C average, but he graduated at the top of his class from Crozer Theological Seminary. Our students frequently do not discover their strengths until the end of their time here or even, like King, until after they have left. I have been amazed at students who come in with academic deficiencies, who upon graduation are accepted into the Ivy League and do very well there, and who frequently become professors in the research universities. The deans and faculty members of the seminaries at Harvard, Boston University, Yale, Union Theological Seminary, the University of Chicago, Princeton, Claremont, Drew, Southern Methodist University, Emory, Howard, Vanderbilt, and Duke tell me that my students usually lead the classes and do exceptionally well. They are good preachers; they are confident and articulate. There is something about being in this affirmative incubator where there are high expectations that changes students forever. In fact, one definition of a racist environment is one of low expectations.

One of our deepest achievements at Morehouse has been to help young men appreciate that when they enter "the House," they are entering a consciousness. In the hieroglyphs, the word *house* means consciousness. They arrive at *More*house. The very name suggests a bigger, more expansive, more liberated state of mind. Across the country, historically, when a student says, "I have been accepted into Morehouse," people respond, "Oh! You are going to the House." That is what they said to me in Boston: "Oh! You are going to the House."

There is a lot of lore around the "Morehouse Mystique." Our seventh president, Hugh Morris Gloster Sr., defined this in terms of academic achievement, professional success, personal integrity, living a life worth emulating, and having a social conscience. It is also more than that. A Morehouse Man is a "man of the House," with a newspaper in one hand, a Bible in the other, and a textbook under his arm. He is always oriented toward service to others and toward leaving the world better than he found it.

"If I can help somebody as I pass along . . . my living will not be in vain."

That was the great song sung at Martin Luther King Jr.'s and Sr.'s funerals by Ebenezer Baptist Church choir member Mary Louise Gurley.

I put a sign on the door to my office that reads, "Servants' Entrance" because Jesus said: "Whoever would be great among you must be your servant, and whoever would be first among you must be your slave; even as the Son of man came not to be served but to serve, and give his life as a ransom for many."[23]

I have dedicated my professional life to Morehouse because I believe in its historical mission, and because I believe that this is the place where I can fulfill the promise I made to myself, Coretta Scott King, and God to keep King's legacy alive. Maybe it is naive to believe that it is possible to create institutions faithful to King's spirit, places that sustain his living and breathing legacy. But I prefer to think hopefully about making a difference. I do not merely hope that it is possible to do this work. I believe that it is necessary.

But sometimes, in order to be true to our historical legacy, we have to be willing to evolve, to meet the demands of history. Sometimes, hewing too closely to our traditions does not preserve who we are; it risks making us irrelevant.

It might seem contradictory, but in my role as a steward of the Morehouse tradition, I have been a harbinger of change. And on a personal level, I have sought to deepen my commitment to my faith and my vocation by striving to grow, by learning from other faith traditions and other scholarly perspectives, and by engaging in other cultures. I have tried to keep this spirit alive at Morehouse College. With the senseless murders of so many African American men and women in the United States, it is necessary to maintain this historically black college, this still all-male campus, relevant in a violent unequal world. I have been charged to do this by the likes of Walter G. Muelder, Marvin C. Griffin, Stephen Joel Trachtenberg, Hugh M. Gloster Sr., Benjamin E. Mays, Coretta Scott King, Howard and Sue Bailey Thurman, Thomas Kilgore Jr., Otis Moss Jr., Harry V. Richardson, Andrew Young, Amos C. Brown, Addie Mitchel, Anne Wimbush Watts, Sylvia and Samuel Du Bois Cook, Wiley A. Perdue, Yvonne King Gloster, and David A. Thomas. These persons and many more at key intersections in my life have reminded me that I can make a decisive difference.

My efforts have not always been understood. Where I see my work as part of a necessary process of revitalization and evolution for the college, others have sometimes felt that I was trying to dilute or divert the mission of the school. I understand their feelings. It has been a challenge for me, growing up as an African American teenager in the 1950s, to continue to grow within today's diverse world, to be willing to see beyond my own understanding of nation, race, culture, and religion and to learn in a truly international, interracial, intercultural, interdisciplanary, and interreligious way.

Although Morehouse is historically a black college, I believe that our school should not be closed to young people of different racial or cultural backgrounds. Benjamin Mays said in his autobiography, *Born to Rebel*, that if Morehouse is not good enough to educate whites, then it is not good enough to educate blacks. The role that the historically black colleges have played in helping to educate and to empower dispossessed people, and to help our nation overcome racial prejudice, has made a significant contribution to making the promise of our nation's founding documents real. I am committed to opening Morehouse and making it more inclusive but not to the extent that we lose sight of the unique meaning of our institution. Staying true to our history and identity is important. Honoring and remembering our historical mission without being blinded by it is essential to charting a path into the future.

Inclusion has to be a process of embracing and respecting the diverse and unique contributions of all people. It cannot be a process of erasing or ignoring or not honoring differences. We must preserve what makes all of us such deep and rich reservoirs of human experience.

Today, we also must be careful of the opposite—holding on too rigidly to what a black college can teach, or to the idea of who our students should be. While we should be proud of our traditions and our history, and always take pride in our unique contributions to our society and to the world, we should also seek to foster a sense of global and cosmic citizenship. As African Americans, embracing our particular history, we should nobly take an equal place in the commonwealth of world citizens and friends. And because our race looks like the rainbow, we should not limit our loyalties and identities to one ethnic group.

It has often been asked, could any of the following multi-generations of Morehouse alumni have graduated from any other American college and achieved and continued to realize the same level of socialized spirituality, social critiques, ethical, legal, educational, healthy effects and transcendent assessment on this nation: Charles Thomas Walker, A.D. Williams, Mordecai Wyatt Johnson, Mark Miles Fisher, Howard Thurman, James Madison Nabrit, William Holmes Borders, Melvin H. Watson, Hugh M. Gloster Sr., Richard I. McKinney, Sandy F. Ray, George D. Kelsey, Charles Radford Lawrence, Horace T. Ward, John H. Ruffin Jr., Edward A. Jones, Martin Luther King Jr. and Sr., Tobe Johnson, Harry S. Wright Sr., Abraham Davis, Maynard Holbrook Jackson Jr., Otis Moss Jr., Lerone Bennett Jr., John H. Hopps,

Wendell P. Whalum, Lonnie King, Julian Bond, Michael L. Lomax, Moses William Howard, Ronald L. Carter, Vincent L. Wimbush, Josiah Young, Robert Michael Franklin, Aaron L. Parker, Harold Dean Tulear, Edward Wheeler, Calvin Otis Butts III, Calvin McLarin, Emerson Harrison, James Earl Davis, Emmett D. Carson, Horace Griffin, Jason Curry, Michael A. Walrond, Delman L. Coates, E. Dewey Smith, Johnny Hill, Echol Nix Jr., Matthew V. Johnson, Charles McKinney, Samuel T. Ross-Lee, Paul Taylor, Eddie S. Glaude Jr., Ronald S. Sullivan, Raphael G. Warnock, Otis Moss III, D. Darrell Griffin, Raynal Harris, Harley Etienne, A. Benjamin Spencer, Jonathan Gayles, David Hefner, Jonathan Walton, Jawanza Colvin, Kelvin R.M. Johnson, Samuel Woodrow William, Floyd B. McKissick Jr., C.K. Steele, Amos C. Brown, Joe Samuel Ratlif, James A. Hudson, Walter E. Massey, Louis W. Sullivan, David Satcher, Samuel Jackson, Shelton J. Spike Lee, Edwin Moses, Claybon Lea Jr., Illya E. Davis, Brandon Thomas Crowley, Willie Francois, Rashad Moore, Nicholas Stuart Richards, Ernst Andrew Brooks, Reginald Sharpe, Winford K. Rice, Stephen Greene, Russel Erich Caufield, and Michael A. Walrond Jr. These men have and are demonstrating the incarnation of founder William Jefferson White's Morehouse communitarian and humanitarian brand in religion, law, medicine, history, philosophy, social ethics, cosmopolitan theology, education, politics, physics, sociology, Biblical studies, and civil and human rights.

To that end, I have tried to foster an international and

ecumenical perspective in our curriculum at Morehouse. I have sought to help our students step out from the confining silos that black colleges risk living in and move toward a broader understanding of what it means to be a person of African descent in a cosmopolitan world.

The perspective of our historically black college can lend something truly valuable to our increasingly multicultural world. As we are beginning to see in places as diverse as Russia and China, India and the European Union, our American struggles to understand our multicultural identity and foster meaningful inclusion contain important lessons for countries around the world facing their own challenges in integrating cultural minorities into their social mainstream.

The challenge of confronting and overcoming racism and prejudice, and the struggle to achieve full inclusion, may be among the most pressing struggles that our nation has faced, but they are not uniquely ours. If we have a role to play as the exemplar to the world of a vibrant and stable democracy, then that role includes showing the world how we have worked to overcome a history of exclusion and prejudice. I believe that Morehouse College, and other historically black schools of higher education, have something valuable to contribute to a broader, global context. Above you see a small but historic and contemporary list of such Morehouse exemplars of transformational leadership.

As I've said, my commitment to this institution also includes the responsibility to be a harbinger of change. I have sought to further my growth by learning from other faith traditions, other scholarly perspectives, and other cultures. The ability to evolve within a changing world is a quality that is essential to Morehouse College, just as it is to any institution that seeks to remain relevant. But the evolution I imagine is not one that causes Morehouse to discard its historical mission but, rather, to use the rich and significant history of this historically black college to address the complex challenges we face today.

The Martin Luther King Jr. International Chapel at Morehouse was built and dedicated in February of 1978. Ambassador Andrew Young flew from the United Nations to deliver the dedication address. The chapel is widely believed to be the most prominent religious memorial in the world dedicated to Martin Luther King Jr. It honors an alumnus who graduated from the college in 1948. He is our best-known graduate. And the work of the chapel is dedicated to globalizing his ideas and ideals.

Upon arriving in Atlanta in 1979 and meeting with President Hugh M. Gloster Sr., he invited me to address the Morehouse board of trustees. My first request was to change the name of the chapel from the Martin Luther King Jr. Memorial Chapel to the Martin Luther King Jr. International Chapel. Why? Because I wanted to render the chapel a clearinghouse for international peace ambassadors and human rights workers from around the world—regardless of nationality, religious creed, color, or sexual orientation. I did not simply want the chapel to be a memorial or a museum for battles no longer being fought. It was my strong desire to have programming that reflected critical discourse around the burning issues in King's last vision of a world house.

The ideas of Martin Luther King Jr. are universally relevant to issues affecting our common humanity. His legacy does not merely belong to African Americans or to the United States. His work has had global impact—in South Africa, Poland, Russia, Chile, Argentina, El Salvador, Denmark, India, China, Mongolia, Eastern Europe, the Philippines, the Intifada, and around the world. The ripples set in motion by his nonviolent approach to social change continue to spread, encouraging people to work toward freedom and democracy.

I made a promise to honor the memory of Martin Luther King Jr. by ensuring that his vision is understood by future generations. This work is not completed by just honoring his name. As an educator, ethicist, pastoral psychologist, and a clinical cosmopolitan theologian, I have made it my life's work to teach the movement he started, the holistic philosophical vision that underlay it, in all of my classes. I also try to do this in my ministry by preaching about the values and virtues that are at the heart of King's vision: the ethical edge of cosmopolitan theology, the black social gospel, nonviolence, compassion, agape love with justice, forgiveness, reconciliation, respect, and peace. I try to live in a way that is true to what this world teacher, this archetype of an educated person, demonstrated to all. In these ways, I have tried to institutionalize and personalize King's legacy.

I founded the Martin Luther King Jr. International Chapel ministry at Morehouse College, a place of collegiate worship that is also a forum to bring people of different cultures, nationalities, and faith traditions together in the spirit of harmony, nonviolence, and peace; in the spirit of critical, controversial, courageous but respectful dialogue; and in the spirit of building Martin Luther King Jr.'s dream of a world house. This is a start toward helping American students who are lagging in familiarity with the international environment understand the meaning of what it is to be a moral cosmopolitan.

Chapter Six

World House

In the early part of my career at Morehouse College there was resistance and a lot of laughter in response to my rhetoric about nonviolence.

"If whitey hits me, he is going to get equal treatment— with interest!" some students would inevitably respond.

I often tell the story in my classes of how a white man approached Dr. King and said to him, "Are you Martin Luther King Jr.?" King answered in the affirmative and the man drew close and spat in his face.

At this point, my students often flip out. They cannot believe anyone would be so disrespectful, and they have a lot of opinions about the right response to such an insult. When I tell them that, on that occasion, King reached very slowly into his back pocket and took out a handkerchief. He wiped the saliva off his face, carefully folded the handkerchief, and handed it to the man, saying, "I think this belongs to you."

The students were astounded—both by the self-control and the cleverness of this response. Last year, though, a rotund, animated young man from a Pentecostal church could not believe it. "If he spat in my face," he said, "it would have been over! I would have hit him!"

That was when the discussion really became animated. I asked my students: "How do you evaluate the effect of Dr. King's response to this man? How do you think it made him feel?"

It was through talking together that they began to see the message in nonviolence and appreciate the wisdom of it. Eventually, I pointed out the obvious: King did not humiliate this man. He did not make him feel less nor did he put him down. King refused to degrade the spitter. He demonstrated that you must separate the deed from the doer—that you must always believe in the higher possibilities for each individual. "If you do not believe that, you cannot be an effective pastor," I added, "because then it means that you do not really have faith in redemption."

After that, we talked about the difference between preaching and practicing. "Are you going to give Jesus lip service, or are you going to do what he said to do?" I asked. "Are you going to be the change you want to see? Because people would rather see a sermon than just hear it."

The young man who had originally been so sure of his response eventually shook his head. "You got me," he admitted.

Ahimsa takes as its basic premise the essential humanity of the opponent. Social change is not accomplished by simply changing an unjust set of laws or an inequitable system. It can only be truly accomplished and secured through human transformation—what Daisaku Ikeda calls "human revolution."

The reasoning is simple: If oppressed people revolt and take over and do to their oppressors what was done to them, nothing has really changed. The social structure remains essentially unjust. The only change is who is on top and who is on the bottom has been reversed. In contrast, the goal of social change through ahimsa is to eliminate the structures of inequality and injustice in relationships between people through a fundamental transformation in how each views the other.

As practiced by King or Gandhi, nonviolent resistance never sought to denigrate those who were in disagreement but rather to elevate them, to touch their higher humanity and arouse in them an awareness of how they were degrading others. Through nonviolent resistance, oppressors were forced to recognize their own inhumanity. In the process, many minds were changed and many hearts were opened. In this way, Gandhi and King sought to elevate an entire society.

For many people, including my students, nonviolent social change is too idealistic to be practical or even effective. In response, I can only point to the fact that Gandhi and King led two of the most important, and successful, social movements in the twentieth century—movements firmly rooted in the practice of nonviolence.

Both Gandhi and King were criticized not just by their opponents. They were also criticized by people who shared their aims but doubted that their methods could achieve results. These critics felt that the urgency of social oppression demanded more forceful action, and many of them advocated violence. To them, using the tools of persuasion and dialogue seemed tantamount to saying that change would be forestalled, possibly forever.

Yet King was acutely aware of the dangers of delay when it came to matters of human justice. He wrote in his famous "Letter From Birmingham City Jail" about black, brown, and yellow brothers of America, Asia, South America, and the Caribbean "moving with a sense of cosmic urgency toward the promised land of racial justice."[24] Change could no longer be slow or incremental. King urged that immediate nonviolent action be taken, and yet, as fierce as the urgency of King's "now" was, he never demanded that change be accomplished by any means necessary.

Awakening the humanity of an opponent can appear impossible. Especially in the context of great civil or human injustice, it can appear that the oppressor is actually evil. But it is at that moment that dedication to forms of resistance that seek to awaken and transform the so-called other through nonviolent means become most important. Nonviolence is easy when your opponent is easily persuadable. It is truly difficult when you feel that your oppressor does not recognize your humanity.

Nonviolence is love and forgiveness in action, and love is justice equally distributed, said King. It is how Jesus lived his life and confronted his would-be enemies. But although King and Gandhi are among the best-known practitioners, nonviolence is not exclusively a Christian or a Hindu philosophy. Gandhi taught that the roots of nonviolence could be found in all of the major religious traditions. It is a universally applicable system of thought and philosophy, of methods and strategies, of art and creativity, grounded in the sacredness of all human personality.

A beloved world community is a moral cosmopolitan commonwealth formed through nonviolent social change. It is formed by people engaged in the earnest struggle to get to know one another. In a beloved community, we understand that we are still progressing toward our highest ideals. We are still growing into a greater understanding of what it is to be human. That elevated sense of what it means to be a human being has not yet arrived in our world, and we must be fiercely committed to helping one another achieve it. To that end, the beloved community provides everyone in the human commonwealth with plenty of space to grow naturally. Some people bloom early and some late. The tragedy is when they do not bloom at all. Therefore, the beloved community stresses patient affirmation. It creates space for all people to blossom.

As King said, we live in a single world house, but as long as we insist on viewing one another through the distancing lens of the nation-state, we cannot face global problems together, nor can we recognize our common humanity, our common good. We must attempt to transcend our differences and to speak to one another as brothers and sisters. We must take the risk of sounding foolish, uninformed, and unpopular to speak to others whose perspectives are different from ours. We cannot risk failing to take actions that we know to be right simply because we fear our motives will be misunderstood.

There is a story from the Gospels that recounts a surprising moment with Jesus. When told by his followers that his mother, sister, and brother had come to see him, he replied, "Who are my mother and my brothers? . . . Whoever does the will of God is my brother and sister and mother."[25]

In my travels, and in my own journey of faith, I have chosen to focus on what I share with others, on compassion, on what makes us family, and not on those things that make us different. In this way, I believe I am acting as Jesus would. I have learned from women and men of many different faith traditions, and while we may use different words for it, I believe we love the same God. I hope never to become convinced that my spiritual learning is so complete that I refuse to learn new ways of love and faith from wise teachers, simply because their vocabulary does not match mine. My Buddhist friends have said yes to their faith, yes to their dharma, yes to the Mystic Law that they embrace. Who am I to say that this Mystic Law is not one of the many names of God? Did not Jesus say, "And other sheep I have, which are not of this fold: them also I must bring, and they shall hear my voice; and there shall be one fold, and one shepherd."[26]

I want to emphasize that creating a beloved community also entails creating the conditions of economic justice, peace, and security here and abroad for women, men, and children. It means ending colonial and neocolonial exploitation. It means eliminating war. These economic agendas were all a part of Martin Luther King Jr.'s larger vision. But at its most fundamental level, his vision was to establish a society founded on empathy and compassion, respect and inclusion. The beloved community is an expression of Christian spiritual ideals. It is the practical application of the teachings of Jesus. These were the concrete goals toward which King aspired. And he spoke of them often.

That the larger sense of King's grand vision is not well known speaks partly to the fact that he was focused so intently on taking action to create immediate social change, and to the immediacy of his fight against poverty, racism, and segregation in American society. He never had time to set forth his ideas in a comprehensive and systematic way. And, of course, this reflects the tragic fact that he was assassinated at the young age of thirty-nine, before he had time to fully articulate his mature theology that transcended narrow disciplinary boundaries and demonstrated the true meaning of philosophy. But we know from what he did write, and from the direction his activism was taking, that this beloved community vision was not only his goal, it was the ethical meaning of the reign of God, of a universal ever-expanding good.

Most of us recall that King first entered the national spotlight as a young man in his mid-twenties when he assumed leadership of the Montgomery Bus Boycott. This was a nonviolent protest that drew national and international attention to the moral evils of segregation in America during the Jim Crow era and, at the same time, set in motion a wave of nonviolent protests, followed by waves of institutional and social desegregation.

In an early article about that boycott, King wrote that it was not integration of public transportation that he sought to accomplish, nor was it even the integration of the public spheres in American society. Rather, what he sought was "reconciliation, redemption, the creation of the beloved community."[27] He sought the transformation of hearts, minds, and attitudes, not just social structures.

Kenneth Smith and Ira Zepp Jr., authors of *Search for the Beloved Community: The Thinking of Martin Luther King Jr.*, say that the beloved community expressed King's vision of "a completely integrated society,"[28] a world where individuals would be allowed to grow to their fullest potential, and where all could live in harmony and thrive, reaching toward our highest innate potential. Ultimately, it meant the creation of "a community of love and justice wherein [humanhood] would be an actuality in all of social life."[29]

Smith and Zepp suggest that for King, this idea was "the ideal corporate expression of the Christian faith,"[30] the literal embodiment in the social and political world of the love and justice at the heart of Christ's teachings.

And if the beloved community was King's ultimate aim, nonviolence was the necessary means to achieve it. For King, the ends could not justify the means; violent or oppressive force could never be a tool for achieving a society founded on Christian love. Love and humanity had to be at the heart of any action taken to achieve meaningful social change, or else the change—however great its ideals—would be betrayed from the start.

In a violent worldview, the ends are deemed important enough that they may justify the use of violent or oppressive means. In the philosophy of ahimsa, however, the ends never justify the means. In fact, we realize that the means and the ends are ultimately the same, because the end must always be preexistent in the means. If we want to accomplish justice, we must behave justly; if we want to see peace, we must behave peaceably; if we want genuine brotherhood among all people, we must treat all people as our brothers and sisters. This is what Gandhi meant when he said, we must "be the change" we wish to see in the world. We cannot have what we are not willing to be.

King describes love as a value common to the major religions of the world. The great spiritual traditions each have lofty theological, philosophical, and doctrinal principles, but in practice, they all teach a single common and human practice.

Love is deeper than doctrine or dogma, more real than theory or theology. Love is not a virtue; it is the norm that makes all virtue possible. It is a force that exists within the human being, something we can summon and exert. This love confers something beautiful upon others. When we love, we ourselves become better. Love ennobles and enriches us.

When I look at the world today, I see religious fundamentalism abroad, and at home, as the source of so much conflict. If the major religious traditions all espouse love, why is there so much violent conflict and oppression, too often in the name of religion? Why is love not practiced more fully in the United States, where the dominant religions have love as their most fundamental tenet? Why, in this country, are we still debating whether to embrace and include people like undocumented immigrants, gay and lesbian Americans, or others who still struggle against the yoke of white supremacy, racism, or disenfranchisement?

When I look at the violent conflicts in the world and the painful struggles of people in our constitutional democracy to claim their full citizenship, I see at work not the redemptive power of religion but the corrosive effect of religious fundamentalism, a distortion of great spiritual teachings and practices into dogmatic exclusivism and rigid rules. This is the negative institutionalization of religion. It hardens teachings, which are flexible and humane, into a set of rules to be obeyed. It turns communities, which were created to affirm and elevate people, into institutions that demand absolute loyalty and fidelity while suppressing, condemning, and demonizing their very humanity.

Toward the end of his final book, *Where Do We Go From Here? Chaos or Community*, King articulated a famous statement:

Today our very survival depends on our ability to stay awake, to adjust to new ideas, to remain vigilant and to face the challenge of change. The large house in which we live demands that we transform this worldwide neighborhood into a worldwide brotherhood. Together we must learn to live as brothers or together we will be forced to perish as fools.[31]

Martin Luther King Jr. made a shift at the end of his life and became even more inclusive. It was as if he was leaving the compass and the map on the kitchen table to guide us on our way.

King felt that, once the Jim Crow laws were off the books and people started to feel like they could use that as a yardstick by which to measure racial equality, some people would park right there and think the work was finished. He wanted them to know that equality was not sufficient if it did not address poverty—if it did not address war.

If he were alive today, I believe King would say mere racial equality does not address the ways in which capitalism has run amok or how it contributes to global warming. How can I know this? Because when he was explaining why he was against the Vietnam War, he talked about the effect of Agent Orange on the crops and on the environment. King had a broader understanding of the ontological horizon. He did not just believe that he could have a personal relationship with the ultimate, with God; he viewed his relationship with all of creation as personal. God was the ultimate person, human beings were penultimate persons, and all the other animals and beings, with one degree or another of consciousness, were different stages and aspects of personhood to a descending level based on the complexity of their conscious organization. This is why King said idealistic personalism was his basic philosophical position.

How does King eventually get to the idea of the world house? He tells us in his "Why I Oppose the War in Vietnam" speech: He discovered that President Lyndon B. Johnson was shifting his attention away from the domestic issues King had raised because he was becoming distracted by the war in Vietnam. King connected some dots and realized Johnson could not give his financial attention to the War on Poverty anymore because this military war was an enormous financial drain. He concluded that until we started to understand the holism of the way we function as a society (that every decision made affects every other decision), we were not going to succeed. Everything was interconnected, and because of that, he could no longer remain silent. He had to lift his voice in opposition to the Vietnam War.

I do not mean to minimize King's dedication to fighting the historical, political, religious, sociological, and structural racial inequality that has always existed in the United States. That was the work for which he gave his life. But for him, this was merely the starting point, the necessary beginning of the work to create this ideal community. He wanted us to transcend that which separates us, that which reinforces our differences and causes us to seek domination over others, and instead to realize that we are living in a great world house. As such, we are all brothers and sisters with responsibilities to care for and love one another, with the aim of making our common planet and our shared human community better and more beautiful, a more perfect union.

For me, this was the highest aim of education. The methods we use to achieve a beloved world community are the same as the methods I would apply in my best pedagogical endeavors—patient education, a commitment to dialogue, and dedicated efforts to find and foster the best in one another. This, then, is how the world house becomes a world family and a global culture of shared traditions.

Chapter Seven

Human Revolution

In my eighteenth year at Morehouse I was exhausted, maybe even burnt out. I had expended a great deal of energy in my efforts to realize Martin Luther King Jr.'s message, and I felt like no one was paying me any attention. I did not have a staff, just a secretary. The Sunday attendance at services was small, only about a hundred people, which seemed smaller than it really was because the chapel seated 2,501. I believed in what I was doing and thought I was in the right place, but I was becoming despondent. A powerful feeling of loneliness had sunk in.

One day I reached the tipping point. I went home, walked in the house, and said to my wife, "I'm leaving."

"Leaving? Where are you going?"

"I do not know," I admitted. "But I'm leaving."

I explained to her how defeated I felt, but she just did not agree with me. "You have everything," she told me. She then had me call her father, who was a prominent Baptist pastor in Texas.

"I do not understand this," he responded on the phone. "You are at the top of your field; you have all these perks. Where else can you go? You are already at the top."

Everything he said rang hollow. I decided to head to an M. Scott Peck's Foundation for Community Encouragement–sponsored conference on the principles of community building near Toronto, which had been recommended by Evelyn Marie Berry, the chapel fundraising consultant. I told my wife that the Lord was going to show me where to go next. Like Abraham, I was hearing the words "Pack. It's traveling time." And like Abraham, I had no idea where I was really going.

The conference did not appear to lead to anything earth-shattering, even though I spent considerable time discussing my concerns with Stephen P. Bauman, senior minister of Christ Church Methodist, New York City, who listened graciously. There were no revelations. I flew to Los Angeles to preach at the Holman United Methodist Church, where they were looking for a new pastor to succeed James Lawson, who had invited Martin Luther King Jr. to Memphis to lead the garbage workers' strike in April 1968. Everything was right that beautiful sunlit Sunday morning—the choir, the orchestra, the organ, the setting, the modern sanctuary, the congregation, and my host, Paul Hill, a classmate of mine at Boston University School of Theology. They loved my sermon and I loved preaching to them. Afterward my friend, who served as liturgist in the service, asked me if I was interested in becoming senior minister at the church. It felt wonderful to receive such an offer, which I did entertain seriously while I greeted the complimenting congregation in the receiving line after the service. But the idea of being under the ecclesiastical authority of a bishop did not set well with me, as I had been licensed and ordained in the prophetic tradition of the freedom of conscience Baptist church, where the authority of the pastor rests with the congregation, not outside the church.

Normally, I would have flown back to Atlanta after that. But something had happened just before I left Morehouse that changed my plans. I was sitting in my office on a hot day. The air conditioning was not working and I was fanning myself with a piece of mail. I was commiserating with my secretary, Muriel E. Brooks, over the fact that I had more bills to pay at the chapel than I had money with which to pay. We had not been in that position before, and I was not sure how we were going to make it. We never had had a deficit during my tenure.

That was when she told me that the Michael Beckwith had called from Los Angeles. Michael had been a student at Morehouse only briefly but had gone on to spiritual prominence as Oprah Winfrey's favorite preacher. An absolutely brilliant leader, I had honored him at King Chapel the previous month. Muriel indicated he had called inviting me to come to visit him on my next trip to Los Angeles, which I thought was rather unusual.

I continued fanning myself and, returning to the matter at hand, said to Muriel: "I have got to pay these bills. But where am I going to get the money to do that?"

"I do not know," she sighed, looking at the stacks of mail on her desk. "Oh, by the way," she added. "Reverend Michael wrote you recently."

"He did? Where is the letter?"

"You are fanning yourself with it!" she laughed.

Sure enough, I looked down at the envelope and it was from the Agape International Spiritual Center, Beckwith's church. I opened it and was stunned to discover a check inside, a donation for a $1,000. "We are saved!" I exclaimed, stunned at this unexpected miracle.

So instead of flying back to Atlanta after my speaking engagement, I stayed in Los Angeles. Michael picked me up on a Wednesday morning at my hotel, and we drove up Highway 1 along the Pacific. We had a wonderful lunch of seafood, walked on the beach, and then drove back to Los Angeles where he showed me some of the places where he had been mentored. The tour ended at Agape, since he had to prepare for the Wednesday evening service.

At Agape, Michael led me through the most impressive church bookstore I had ever seen. When I asked him to suggest a book, he handed me *Words That Heal Today* by Ernest Holmes. Little did I know that it would turn out to be the best book I had ever read on Jesus, a game-changer of a book for me. Meeting with Michael Beckwith was also a game-changer.

As we walked through the lobby together, crowds of people were coming into the sanctuary, where he seated me in the second row. I could feel a lot of excitement in the air. The music was spirited, and when he began to preach I was blown away. He used no notes. Later, when I brought some of my friends from the SGI to hear him, they too were impressed.

As Michael finished preaching, I took a deep breath. Something had happened! I barely even knew where I was. He started introducing his guests in the congregation and then, without any warning at all, he announced, "I'm going to have Dr. Carter from Morehouse College come up to greet and meet you."

I rose and had no idea what I was going to say but walked confidently onto the platform. As I stood at the lectern, I looked over at Michael and he had this satisfied Mona Lisa smirk on his face. I looked out at the warm congregation. It was integrated in every possible manner. This was the world house.

Something happened that night at Agape, and afterward I would never be the same. Everybody in that church knew that something had happened, and they knew it had happened to me. I had to catch a plane but did not want to leave. I knew that this was a decisive turning point in my life.

From Los Angeles International Airport I flew to Toronto because I had learned that Colgate Rochester Crozer Divinity School was looking for a new president. I felt led to walk the grounds to see if I sensed a new calling away from Morehouse. I rented a car and drove by Niagara Falls. The roar of those waters was frightening—I had never seen anything like it in my life. And yet, I felt like I was supposed to be standing before it, feeling the spray of those powerful waters on my face. I returned to the car and drove over to the school, walked around the campus, into the classrooms and the chapel where I once preached at the invitation of Dean Robert Michael Franklin, visited the American Baptist Archive, and tried to discern from Spirit's presence or discern whether this was where I was supposed to be. But nothing came to me. I spent several hours at the George Eastman Museum feeling out the spirit of the city of Rochester.

I arrived home in the early afternoon on Sunday. My wife was the organist at the historic Ebenezer Baptist Church and could not transport me, so one of the deacons met me at the airport instead. I had shopping bags of materials, cassettes, and books I had purchased at the Agape bookstore. I came in the house and started moving everything in—the luggage, the bags, the gifts. I said goodbye to the deacon and started taking things inside the house to my basement study. I had one more shopping bag, one more trip. I picked it up and started downstairs—and I stumbled. I tripped. I fell all the way down the steps.

I can count the times I have fallen on one hand with fingers left over. This was the worst fall I have ever had in my life. The shopping bag of cassettes and books went everywhere. When I reached the bottom of the steps, I was stunned, feeling my legs must be bent into the shape of pretzels. I did not move. I was afraid I had broken something. I looked up the steps and from the top to the bottom everything I was carrying was strewn on the stairs. I could not believe this had happened to me. I had traveled a great distance, back and forth across the country, and had not had any mishaps.

But as I was lying on the floor looking up, I saw an image. It was an angel-like figure with wings, but it had Michael's face. And he was laughing. "I told you that getting what you want would cost you something." Then he disappeared. The moment I moved I felt a pain in my right ankle and thought of how Jacob limped after wrestling with the angel.

I could not let my wife see me in this condition, so I hobbled around and picked everything up, then drove myself to the emergency room of the Crawford Long Hospital listening to a cassette of Rickie Byars Beckwith's Agape Choir. The nurse joked with me, telling me my ankle was crying, saying, "You hurt me!" But it was not broken and they wrapped it and gave me crutches, after which I drove home, singing with the Agape Choir,

I release and I let go,
I let the Spirit run my life.
And my heart is open wide,
Yes, I'm only here for God.
No more struggle, no more strife,
With my faith I see the light.
I am free in the Spirit,
Yes, I am only here for God.

Muriel was standing in my office doorway when I arrived at Morehouse the next day. As we were catching up, I noticed a strange expression on her face. "Is there something wrong?" I asked.

"Oh no," she said.

"Are you sure?"

"Everything's fine," she said, the hint of a smile on her lips.

"But the way you are looking at me . . ."

"Well," she admitted at last. "You're different, that's all."

"Different bad or different good?"

"It's good!" she said. "You don't seem, well, as pushy as you used to be."

And that is how it started. Everywhere I went on the campus people who would normally not speak to me crossed the street to walk next to me. Faculty members stopped me and said: "You really look good. What are you doing? Did you lose weight?"

I had thought I needed to change my job, but what I had changed was something inside myself. I had experienced my awakening, my own human revolution. I no longer brought prepared remarks with me to the pulpit on Sundays, but after my first sermon that fall, one of the English professors, Anne Wimbush Watts, passed a handwritten note to my wife, which said, "Your husband is a spiritual genius." The president of the college, Walter Massey, was stunned as well—and he was a physicist, maybe an atheist who did not believe in anything he could not prove. Still he placed a phone call to the executive committee of the board of trustees and said, "Something in Dean Carter has changed."

"Is that good?" the trustees wanted to know.

"It's wonderful," said the president.

Morehouse College did not change. I changed. I was no

longer as worried about the chapel. I was home and I was not interested in leaving anymore.

But while I was happy at Morehouse, I felt more than ever that my orthodox Baptist Christianity was not addressing my needs. I felt alone and not really supported by my denomination in the building of my ministry.

Not that the Baptists have not supported me financially. The National Baptist Convention USA Inc. gave me the money to place the statue of Martin Luther King Jr. on the King Chapel plaza—the only such statue in Georgia for more than thirty years. I have represented them at ecumenical meetings as a member of the governing board of the National Council of Churches of Christ for seven years, and I have visited other countries on their behalf. Many Baptist preachers have been to the Martin Luther King Jr. International Chapel to preach. But the National Baptist Convention USA Inc. does not affirm women preachers and are against the Supreme Court decision in favor of same-gender loving marriages.

Worst of all, there is a great deal of egotistical pomposity among the clergy. I used to spend Sunday mornings visiting different churches, since my services were in the evenings. But I stopped attending because I was not gaining anything from the experience. Everything was hackneyed, stuck in simplistic statements that had lost their profundity. "The Garden of Eden was populated with Adam and Eve, not Adam and Steve," I would hear, as if that was enough to justify discrimination against gays. I was amazed at the lack of leadership Baptist pastors were giving to the issue. One of my most prominent students, Delman L. Coates, a Harvard scholar (with a PhD from Columbia University in New Testament and Early Christianity), was demonized for his interpretation of Scripture in a way that supported gay rights. He was punished by the clergy of the Hampton Ministers Conference for giving voice to a more progressive affirmative stance that actually agreed with President Barack Obama and the Supreme Court's position on gay marriage and the civic virtue of equality in which love wins by being legally sanctioned at the highest federal level. No one should participate in the demonization of virtue, least of all self-acknowledged ordained Baptist followers of Jesus.

When I met with Michael Beckwith and began to learn about the New Thought Ancient Wisdom community, and as I learned about the Soka Gakkai International, I found spiritual communities that did not hide behind degrees, titles, or fancy cars. They were much more interested in practicing than in preaching; more interested in being the thing itself than just talking about it. To me that seemed to be the meaning of following Christ. They breathed humanity into my Christianity.

I have always maintained a belief in the inherent dignity of human personality, but many people at Morehouse were concerned with maintaining political respectability, and this created a cultural sameness that did not always respect everyone's individuality and difference. I sensed that many Morehouse alumni never wanted me to use Martin Luther

King Jr.'s stance on embracing the so-called other as a justification of the acceptance of diversity. In the twentieth century, the issue was civil rights and ending segregation, and Morehouse was in the forefront of producing the leaders that brought about that change. Now the hurdles were diversity, difference, inclusion, and pluralism, and we could not be a leader in this new millennium if we stayed in the pristine glory of the past while overlooking discrimination of any kind in the present. That would be a violation of the symbolic significance of King's statue on the chapel plaza.

As I reflect on my life, I can say with humility that it has been rich, and I have been true to the vocation to which I was called. I have tried to embody the values of global learning and interfaith understanding in my work. That has not been easy. Not only have I bumped up against the limits of my knowledge and abilities, I have also faced the challenges of a demanding professional life and the obligations of faith, friends, family, fans, facilitators, filibusters, fanatics, fakes, freaks, flamboyance, fools, and fellow travelers. This is not an excuse; it is a simple statement of fact. I have not done all I set out to do. So when I encounter people who have done remarkable things—people whose lives and responsibilities are no less demanding than mine—I am impressed, and I know I have something to learn from them.

The amazing technological advances of the twentieth and twenty-first centuries have not led to quantum leaps in the basic respect of people for one another. Violence of all kinds proliferates—ethnic, economic, environmental, racial, religious, interpersonal, and intimate. And we are not just spectators. We are a part of the problem of all that violence, and a part of the solution. We must not live in a fantasy world but must be realistic and hopeful, accepting our complicity in violence and taking responsibility too.

It is popular to blame other people for what is wrong in the world. We blame our family, the center, the church, the cathedral, the mosque, the synagogue, the temple, the Scriptures, the government, global capitalism, our genes, or our environment. We need a clear analysis of the influences these factors have in creating a violent world. But there are no excuses for not accepting responsibility for ourselves.

We need an alternative vision, a humane alternative to violence like the ones offered by Mahatma Gandhi, by Martin King and, as I was learning, by Daisaku Ikeda, a moral cosmopolitan spiritual genius.

Every living planetary citizen is now charged to make certain that the victims of global atrocities—such as the Christian Crusades; the slaughter of the Native Americans; the savagery of the African slave trade; the Middle Passage and the aftermath of black deaths brought on in the United States from a culture of deep racism and easy legal access to guns; the Holocaust; the genocides of Cambodians, Rwandans, and others; the dropping of the atomic bombs on Hiroshima and Nagasaki, Japan; the Indian Hindu–Pakistani Muslim slaughter of 1947, which stabbed Gandhi in the heart on the eve of his greatest nonviolent victory; the murder of four little girls at Sunday school in a Birmingham church and the nine at a prayer meeting in a Charleston church; the secret slayings during apartheid in South Africa; the 9/11 attacks; the March 22, 2003, American "shock and awe" campaign in Iraq with its "collateral damage"; or any other unspeakable violence—did not die in vain.

The disease of violence is progressive—and is terminal—but is not incurable. Once infected, individuals can recover. Many people have turned away from lives of violence. Societies can recover as well. We must seek to inculcate within ourselves a nonviolent consciousness.

Violence is not inevitable! Human beings are responsible. We make choices. All of us are choosing our way into our future. Each of us is one decision away from heaven or hell, to being a blessing to the world or a curse.

It can be difficult for my students to understand this, particularly the Pentecostals and the Baptists. Once I was talking to a crowded classroom, speaking Carter-ology, and I said, as I believe: "There is no Devil. You cannot have two ultimates in the universe. It's a universe, not a dual-verse."

"No!" shouted a young man sitting over to the side. "No! That's not right!'

A hush came over the room. Nobody had ever seen anybody speak to me like that. He was an articulate young man from San Antonio, Texas, Renard Darnell Allen Jr., from a long line of preachers, but he did not know that he was espousing white Southern Baptist fundamentalist theology. He needed the Devil in his life. He needed an "other," an enemy, an objective evil. I let him rant while everyone in the room froze. He was verbally attacking the dean of the Martin Luther King Jr. International Chapel, and that kind of disrespect was frightening to the other students. Everyone was staring at him and then staring at me wondering what was going to happen next.

I let him get all his arguments out.

When he finally finished with all of the orthodox, traditional Baptist doctrines, I was initially silent, unsure of what approach to take. I turned and walked out of the chapel library into my office and pulled Elaine Pagels's *The Origin of Satan* off the shelf. When I came back into the room, I handed it to him.

I explained my action to the room full of chapel assistants, many of them future seminarians. Elaine Pagels has been the Harrington Spear Paine Foundation Professor of Religion at Princeton University since 1982. She received her PhD in religion from Harvard University and reads and writes all of the languages relevant to the academic study of the Gospels. She is an authority on the similarities between the Pauline Epistles, Gnosticism, and Buddhism. Her 1979 book, *The Gnostic Gospels*, examines the divisions in the early Christian church and the way women have been treated throughout Jewish and Christian history. Modern Library named *The Gnostic Gospels* one of the hundred best books of the twentieth century. She's written on the origin of Satan and documents how the New Testament writers borrowed this concept from the Old Testament as a way to describe as evil those who rejected

Jesus. In other words, Pagels argues that Satan served to "confirm for Christians their own identification with God and to demonize their opponents—first other Jews, then pagans, and later dissident Christians called heretics."[32] I turned to the irate young man, handed him the book, and said, "You will find my response to your objections in Pagels's book."

A week later he returned—and apologized to me in front of all the chapel assistants. At a much later date they elected Renard president of this organization.

Now everyone else wanted to know what was in that book, and it became a remarkable teaching opportunity. We began a very interesting dialogue among the chapel assistants because I had demonstrated nonviolence in a hostile situation. I did not lecture Renard. I did not reprimand or reject him. I gave him an assignment in a thinking community to prepare him to engage in a future dialogue from a position of intellectual strength. Eventually he graduated from the San Francisco Theological Seminary and went on to be senior pastor of the St. Luke Baptist Church in Dayton, Ohio.

We cannot have what we are not willing to be. Peace, harmony, and the beloved community are everywhere, except where we are blocking them in our lives. The way to heal every situation is to begin by becoming spiritually aware of humanity's potential. We must believe that our culture of violence can be transformed into a culture of peace. Let us do this in the hallowed name and sacred memory of all the children, youth and young adults, women, and men worldwide whose humanity was not respected by religion over the ages.

Everything that I am doing today has as its goal global peace. But you must understand how this runs against black religiosity, because the majority of those in the Southern Baptist Convention firmly believe that people cannot bring peace to the world. They believe peace will only come when Jesus returns. Therefore, when you join the church and are baptized, you are only at first base. You hit the ball, you get a run, and you make it to first base. Then you run to the dugout and sit down and look at the sky and wait for the Parousia, the Second Coming of Jesus. They do not believe you are to play the entire game! They do not understand that being like Christ, working for the ultimate reign of God by doing the will of God and working for the beloved community, means bringing about peace on earth by being peace itself.

The church has never made it clear that this is the goal, and the best proof is the fact that most church members have never heard a sermon on peace. Preachers do not preach on peace! It is amazing. A dissertation was written at Boston University on sermons preached in the south by black pastors and white ministers on the Sunday after King's assassination. The survey revealed that the white preachers took their text from the New Testament and Christ's teachings, while the black preachers took their text from the Old Testament with its commandments and judgments and story of the Hebrew Exodus.

Martin Luther King Jr.'s practice of cosmopolitan Christianity and Mahatma Gandhi's original practice of nonviolent Hinduism tell us that there is another way of looking at human nature. It is the same position taken by the Psalmist who declares humanity to be the highest product of God's creativity (Psalm 8). If human beings are made in God's image, are we not then entitled to look for expressions of the divine in our makeup?

When I first began reading about the SGI, I realized that it was a form of peace-oriented resistance based on agape. It offered an alternative vision of our interdependence and our diversity, a revolutionary vision of inclusive forgiveness and of personal and communal dignity. Furthermore, Ikeda was not warden to the prison of conventional morality. As I learned about him, I quickly realized that he has done a much more effective job at institutionalizing his message and his dreams than even Gandhi or King.

When I met Ikeda and came to learn of his accomplishments, I felt so inspired. I know from my own experience how challenging it is to create organizational and institutional structures, mechanisms, and instruments with a genuine global vision. I appreciated the scale of his accomplishments, not just because I agreed with their aims, but because I understood the difficulties he no doubt faced along the way.

There are not many people who embody a true and deep world perspective and a global interfaith understanding that are respectful of differences. Ikeda is certainly such a person. There are not many men who can claim accomplishments in so many different realms—in spiritual leadership, in advocacy for peace and human rights, and, most importantly, in education—but Ikeda is certainly such a man, who as a spiritual leader has a vision of the steps needed for moving the world toward realizing global peace, which he calls *kosen-rufu*.

He will have disciples for peace for many generations to come. He is inspiring them, he is educating them, and he is giving them the tools to create peace within themselves and in the world. This was why I felt so dedicated to him from the start. I saw in him the long shadow of Gandhi and King. Daisaku Ikeda was saying what I believe Mahatma Gandhi and Martin King would be saying if they were alive today.

Chapter Eight

Buddhist Teacher

I am thirteen years younger than Daisaku Ikeda, and our experiences during World War II were necessarily different. Children in the continental United States did not experience air raids. Compared to children living in Japanese cities, we were comparatively safe and secure. But in spite of these differences, I identify profoundly with Daisaku Ikeda—with his inextinguishable passion for peace.

Ikeda was thirteen when President Franklin D. Roosevelt made the declaration on December 8, 1941, before a joint session of Congress that Americans had been dreading but that the attacks on Pearl Harbor made inevitable: The United States of America was at war with the Empire of Japan. All four of Ikeda's older brothers were marched off to battle. He witnessed the effect that his eldest brother's death in Burma had on his mother, and to this day it remains one of the most painful memories of his life.

His mother worked hard to remain in seeming good cheer, humming as she went about her chores to keep up the spirits of everyone else in the house. An entire year passed by with no word from her sons. She continued to hum even so, stoically. Meanwhile, the family's modest home was demolished twice, the second time by fire bombs that fell at night, forcing them to live in a sheet metal hut. Ikeda's mother kept humming; she kept hoping. Frail as a child, Ikeda perspired profusely through the nights, his lungs wheezing with tuberculosis. His father also took ill. Pitifully poor, he writes, "All that remained for those in our wasted city was the increasing difficulty of finding enough to eat."[33] Ikeda's brother Kiichi never returned. In January 1945, seven months before the wretched war's end, he was killed.

Because Japan's resources were given over to waging a futile war, Ikeda experienced poverty, ill health, and malnourishment. He saw homes, communities, and families destroyed. And he saw how his own family suffered because of this war. All of these experiences inspired his lifelong dedication to eradicating war.

Ikeda certainly understands that there are many different justifications for war, some more noble and some more base. But to him, there is no such thing as a just war. There is no cause that warrants the cost to human life, nothing that justifies the devastation of families, homes, and communities, or to the natural world. I believe anyone who has lived through war, anyone who has personally experienced it, can understand how strongly Ikeda feels. I know that I do. Ikeda understands the primacy of what Peter A. Bertocci called "the essence of a person," when he writes:

The SGI's efforts to grapple with the nuclear weapons issue are based on the recognition that the very existence of these weapons represents the ultimate negation of the dignity of life. It is necessary to challenge the underlying inhumanity of the idea that the needs of states can justify the sacrifice of untold numbers of human lives and disruption of the global ecology. At the same time, we feel that nuclear weapons serve as a prism through which to bring into sharper focus ecological integrity, economic development, and human rights—issues that our contemporary world cannot afford to ignore. This in turn helps us identify the elements that will shape the contours of a new, sustainable society, one in which all people can live in dignity.[34]

In other ways, too, I recognized my own values and ideals in Ikeda.

I was raised as an African American man at a time in American history when we were not expected to do great things. Ikeda came from a humble family of seaweed harvesters in Tokyo and had few educational opportunities. But that did not stop him from reading and learning. He was blessed to encounter a great teacher, Josei Toda, and to work closely with him for more than a decade. That relationship changed his life in much the same way that my encounter with Martin Luther King Jr. changed mine. We have not had the advantages of other people. And yet, we have dedicated our lives to work we felt was important, and because of that we have been able to utilize opportunities that we made for ourselves. We share similar hopes for a better and more humane world.

I traveled to Japan for the first time in September 2000. Ikeda had invited me to speak at Soka University, the educational institution he founded just outside of Tokyo. Before I left, I read a speech he had given to the students there, and I was surprised that he devoted much of it to the history of Morehouse College, particularly the lives of Martin Luther King Jr. and Benjamin Elijah Mays, the sixth president of Morehouse, whom King regarded as his mentor. Ikeda even quoted at length from a book I edited, *Walking Integrity*, that honored the Mays legacy. I was powerfully moved. It was clear that just as I had been studying his work and learning about his accomplishments, Ikeda had been studying my work and the issues that mattered to me.

When I arrived at Soka University of Japan, I was not sure when I was going to meet Ikeda himself. I imagined that eventually someone would usher me down a hallway and into his office. Instead, after an extensive tour of a large exhibition on Ikeda's life and achievements, I was ushered onto a full elevator and it stopped, presumably to let on other passengers. I was only half conscious of this, however, because I was looking down at the speech I was planning to give. When the doors remained open a bit longer than expected, I finally looked up and there were as many people outside the elevator as on it, all pressed together like sardines in a can. I did not know anybody and was looking around through this swirl of humanity wondering when I would meet Ikeda. Then I felt someone pulling at my arm; it was Ikeda himself reaching into the elevator and pulling me out of it.

Things happened quickly. He led me into the space outside of the elevator, and with every step we took that space became larger and wider until it became the actual stage of the auditorium in Makiguchi Hall—and it was packed to the gills! I had already been welcomed by a choir singing "We Shall Overcome," and when they finished, they broke out into the Morehouse hymn. Everyone in the choir was wearing a Morehouse T-shirt. I was blown away!

This entrance onto the Makiguchi stage, however, was the zenith of my life. Everyone was applauding, cheering, smiling, and I was taking it in, absorbing everything and thinking, "If my mother could see me now!" There was a band playing and photographers were everywhere. When I finished speaking and took my seat, my escort leaned over to me and said, "While you were speaking you were being broadcast to a thousand SGI centers throughout Japan, and when you leave this building you will be a celebrity all over Japan."

After all the speeches had been given and the big crowds had dispersed, I met with Ikeda and his wife, Kaneko, along with our translators in a small room. He took his coat off, relaxed in his shirtsleeves, and began asking many questions. His queries included matters related to my background, my mother, where I was born, where I went to school, what my educational experiences had been, and the like.

Ikeda asked about my first meeting with Martin Luther King Jr., and as we talked about that encounter, he was particularly interested in hearing about King's humanity and the quality of his personality. Unlike many others I have told about this encounter, Ikeda did not simply want to discuss my commitment to King's values or our shared faith. He wanted to understand the personal basis for the significant regard I hold for my mentor—why I had given my life to his teachings. The best way to fulfill Jesus's words "Thy kingdom come, Thy will be done, On earth as it is in heaven"[35] is to realize King's moral cosmopolitan dream. King's search for common ground to help create the ultimate beloved economic world community is the ethical meaning of the presence of God. This is the vortex of my commitment to King's values and our shared faith in humanity's unlimited possibilities. Ikeda asked about King's famous "I Have a Dream" speech and why I thought this speech resonated so effectively as the emblem of the American Civil Rights Movement. Why had that speech continued to speak to people around the world today, calling them together in the struggle for human freedom?

I had not thought much about that question before, but I realized as I answered it that it was not simply the power of King's language and oratory that was so effective, nor was it just the historical significance of that March on Washington. It was because those words welled forth from the depths of King's being, because they echoed the hopes and dreams of generations long gone. It was those ancestral hopes and dreams, and the vision for a future where they could be realized, that gave that speech its true, enduring power.

Ikeda then asked me to describe where I was when King was assassinated, and how I felt at that moment. That was a profoundly personal question, and answering it, I had to describe an emotionally difficult moment in my life to a person I had just met. But I did it. I shared with him just how traumatic it was to lose the man I most admired to a bigoted act of violence. I told him how hard it was to stay true to King's ideals—to turn away from hatred, bitterness, and anger toward compassion, forgiveness, and agape.

I have to be honest. Because of the size of the Soka Gakkai in Japan, with its millions of members, and because Ikeda is so well known there as to be a household name, I expected the meeting to be formal and ceremonial. I had assumed Ikeda would use the occasion to tell me about himself and his achievements, or possibly discuss how we might be able to work together. Instead, he spent most of the time asking about me. I was impressed at how much he already knew about my life but also at how humble and genuine he was in getting to know me better.

One question in particular really struck me. Ikeda shared his great concern for the increasing incidences of youth violence in Japan. He asked my thoughts about such violence in the United States. At one point he turned to me with sudden intensity and asked, "How should adults inter-act with children who are driven to violence?"

After much thought I answered, "The only way to solve youth violence is for adults to actively demonstrate the power of nonviolence."

The media is saturated with violence, and even our political leaders speak disrespectfully of people with whom they are in disagreement. They often advocate harsh, con-frontational, and violent methods against such people. The very language they use is violent and degrades the human-ity of those with whom they disagree. This affects our polit-ical discourse, but it also affects our national culture.

Children learn from adults, especially from our behav-ior when we think they are not engaged or paying atten-tion. If we want to address the problem of violence among our young, we have to be willing to bear responsibility for the kind of values and behavior we model for our children. Popular entertainment is overwhelmingly violent, and when we as adults glorify violence, it is not surprising that young people think that violence is an acceptable way to resolve conflict.

In Ikeda's case and mine, our families were instrumen-tal in sheltering us from hardships as best they could, shep-herding us through hard times while showing us the value of faith and fortitude. We were like all young people, learn-ing more by observing the behavior of our parents than we could have learned from any sermon. Practice is more pow-erful than preaching, and example is more powerful than words. Youth will always do what you do but not necessarily what you say to do.

Ikeda explained his belief that "education must give young people the power to liberate themselves and to show them how to grow into mature self-actualizing adults who possess diverse talents." As someone whose whole life has been devoted to the transforming power of education, I could not help agreeing with him.

At one point in our conversation, I recalled that when Martin King was asked to name the foremost Christian of the twentieth century, he named Mahatma Gandhi, who was, in fact, not a Christian. I told Ikeda that King had a broad and encompassing view of Christianity. He embraced anyone with whom he found common cause, regardless of their religious faith.

In fact, Gandhi was an Indian Jain Hindu who, while practicing an original version of Hinduism, was nevertheless widely read in all other religions and known for integrating Christian hymns, prayer, rituals, Scriptures, even the Nichiren Buddhist chant into his own spiritual practice. Like King, he was open to receiving wisdom from other traditions. And, of course, both King and Gandhi acknowledged that they were tutored on "civil disobedience" and nonviolence by an American white man, Henry David Thoreau, a key figure in the transcendentalist movement, which was influenced by the work of a French woman, Madame Anne Louise Germaine de Stael-Holstein, mostly known as Madame Germaine de Stael, who herself was introduced to transcendentalism by German philosophers.

Every one of these great leaders, in order to find the deeper pattern that unites us across all boundaries, had to transcend the expectations and limitations of race, nationality, religion, language, gender, and culture. This meant they had tapped into a subterranean river of wisdom that runs beneath all of those traditions.

It was a memorable dialogue and I have been honored to have more such conversations with Ikeda, whom I found to be a free, kind, learned, and committed person. After our talk, I was inspired, affirmed, motivated, and edified. I remember thinking, "This is a man with whom I can work and become friends." We were raised in different countries—raised, in fact, in nations at war with each other—and still our experiences had so much good in common.

Ikeda took copious notes on our conversation. I was so struck by that. What I sensed most from him was a tremendous sincerity, unpretentious, open and honest, with no ego at all. He seemed to be coming from a place of such profound nonviolence, humility, and concern for humanity that even after spending a relatively brief time with him, I felt heard, seen, known, and whole. I was at peace.

Luckily, when I began to hear of the skepticism with which some of my academic colleagues regarded Ikeda and the SGI, I had already begun to formulate my own opinions. I know better than to be easily swayed by an unreflective and uniformed street committee. And, to be honest, I know something of how visionary thinkers and leaders are misunderstood. Their motives are often misrepresented, and their followers are frequently labeled as fanatical or dangerous. This may be especially true when it comes to Americans having to render extra consideration to the Japanese, not to mention Buddhists. Perhaps it's the result of the vestigial remains of resentment over Pearl Harbor in the American psyche. But, for the record, I lost a maternal uncle, Curtis Childs, in the Japanese attack on Pearl Harbor. I have forgiven the Japanese.

Any African American alive during the nonviolent Civil Rights Movement—in fact, any committed person of any race who was engaged in that struggle—would understand how such misunderstandings arise. Sometimes negative press just means that someone is making waves, and this is not always a bad thing. I try to withhold judgment until I can learn for myself about the real substance of a man, a woman, or a movement.

I have seen ample evidence of the good work of the SGI, the good hearts of its members, and the caring leadership of its president. My continued commitment to the SGI for nearly two decades has only strengthened my determination to work with them toward global peace. Some have been suspicious of me, asking what common cause a black scholar, a Baptist preacher, and an avowed Christian follower of Jesus could find with a Japanese-based lay Buddhist community that does not even worship God.

I have had to ask myself many questions as well. Is the SGI's interpretation of the teachings of the historical Buddha more adaptive than accurate? Why do so many

African Americans, traditionally diehard Christians who lean toward fundamentalism, find Nichiren Buddhism so appealing? How is it that SGI practitioners have developed such a deep connection to Daisaku Ikeda, even though he does not speak English and rarely visits America? In fact, Ikeda has never seen the world-class institution known as Soka University of America in Aliso Viejo, California, which he founded. Is the SGI merely a cult of personality since practitioners embrace Ikeda, a man that most have never met, as their mentor in life and enthusiastically promote his work and writings?

In my search to find answers to these and many other questions, I have found in lay Nichiren Buddhism, Daisaku Ikeda, and the *kosen-rufu* movement he leads an authentic religious philosophy and spiritual practice that mirrors the core beliefs, spiritual values, and democratic ideals of my own mentor, Martin Luther King Jr. But, unlike King, Ikeda is one who walks among us. Although he is over ninety, he is still here, showing the way to be peace itself. It is Ikeda who helped me to see even more clearly that the essence of King's philosophy was his conviction that peace is not only possible, but plausible. Upon recovering this wisdom from him, I became more aware as a Christian theist of my own yearning for peace as a viable outcome to the world's conflicts.

Nevertheless, as a trained scholar, I first listened to the critics and examined the published literature. As I reviewed the scholarship about the SGI, I discovered that while there was certainly a great deal of initial skepticism about the SGI, over time this has changed. In the past two decades, media coverage of the Soka Gakkai in Japan and SGI in the West has become more balanced, and academic scholarship has become more open to learning from its astonishing growth, its world class contributions, assessing what this movement has done in galvanizing popular involvement, and identifying where its earlier methods of proselyting were excessive.

The Soka Gakkai is a wealthy and powerful organization in Japan, but so are many of the major religious organizations in the United States. The Komeito (Clean Government Party), the political party that Ikeda founded in Japan, was funded initially by the Soka Gakkai, and its first candidates elected to office were adherents to their faith. But it has been an independent political organization for many decades now. Ikeda certainly speaks out on political matters, using his public stature to advocate on behalf of issues such as strengthening the United Nations or calling for nuclear disarmament. But religious figures and organizations in the United States also act in the political realm, and it seems clear that Ikeda's political positions are consistent with his Buddhist ethics and global values. Moreover, while I cannot speak to any supposed political ambitions that Ikeda might ever have had, I believe that if he had them, he would have (and could have) acted to accomplish them long ago. At this stage of his life, he seems to be more focused on leaving behind a solid foundation for the religious, educational, and cultural institutions he's founded, and to completing his legacy through his writing.

King and Gandhi did not have as much effect on the United Nations as Ikeda has had. He is a good role model of how to negotiate the structures of civil institutions. Particularly impressive is how he responded to the Nichiren Shoshu Buddhist priesthood, with which Soka Gakkai was affiliated for decades. The priests, though they benefited for years from Soka Gakkai members' donations, always felt superior to and even resented the growth of the lay movement. In the early 1990s, they excommunicated the Soka Gakkai in a ploy to gain control of the membership. The effort failed, with the vast majority of Soka Gakkai members feeling that they had finally been liberated from an archaic and authoritarian priesthood.

In a later act of spite, the priesthood tore down their own Grand Main Temple in 1998. This extraordinary modernist architectural structure was built with funds raised almost exclusively by the SGI's worldwide membership and was at that time the pride of the movement. For SGI members, who gave $100 million to build it, the Grand Main Temple's demolition was like losing their Vatican. The renegade Nichiren Shoshu priests spent some $35 million tearing down the temple at the foot of Mount Fuji. And yet, throughout it all, Ikeda was the epitome of Gandhian and Kingian nonviolence. The way Ikeda continued his ministry in the face of this arrogant, authoritarian, hostile, and anti-spiritual demolition, carried out by the Nichiren Shoshu priesthood against the protests of hosts of internationally acclaimed architects, not to mention the SGI's twelve million members, was impressive. No wonder there is so much disrespect for clergy the world over. Ikeda was not deterred, even in the face of a weak Japanese judicial system that refused even to investigate the event.

Initially, this schism with the priesthood, which effectively left the organization without a clergy, was hard for a preacher like me to fathom. But eventually I saw it as an evolutionary and revolutionary advance in the history of world religion. With his emphasis on education, dialogue, human revolution, and a culture of peace, Ikeda has given the members of the SGI the tools to practice nonviolence and realize a sustainable, cosmic harmony. Eventually, I came to understand that Ikeda was also offering other religions the methods to revitalize their own communities— and to find ways of being together that were closer to the original practices of early Christians.

I can say unequivocally that of all the spiritual and philosophical leaders I have met—many of them the twentieth century's most revered—it is this Japanese lay Buddhist, still unknown to many outside of his native country, who has been the most impressive in terms of sincerity, learning, action, integrity, achievement, and global vision. Daisaku Ikeda has captured my heart, my mind, and my spirit in a way that I find difficult to describe—except to say that at last, after many years, I have found another mentor.

Chapter Nine

The Power of Moral Cosmopolitan Dialogue

One of the unique features of the Soka Gakkai International—both today and in 1947, when the nineteen-year-old Daisaku Ikeda first met his mentor, Josei Toda—is that they congregate primarily in semi-formal discussions held in one another's homes. While the SGI has many centers of varying sizes throughout the world, its members do not view those centers the same way that most Christians might view their local church edifices. Many events or activities are held at the SGI centers, but the basic place where the members congregate is in these house meetings. This is reminiscent of how early Christians met in the homes of the followers of the Way after they were expelled from the Jewish Synagogue, sixty-three years after Jesus's ascension.

These discussion meetings, as they are known, are one of the most interesting features of the SGI. The primary congregational emphasis of the SGI rests not on any temple or church or monastery or mosque or synagogue or center, but on small group gatherings in the homes of practitioners. I believe that this is, at least in part, because the SGI is a lay-based movement. Gathering in formal temples or churches confers a special power on the clerical authority residing in those sanctuaries and speaking from those pulpits. Gathering in people's homes seems, by contrast, inherently populist and democratic, with everyone informally dressed. I have come to appreciate it as a deceptively simple expression of the inherent egalitarianism of the SGI.

Members of the SGI conduct their traditional chanting form of worship when they gather. But their gatherings are conducted by fellow believers, not by clergy wearing robes and conducting ceremonial rituals. After their communal worship, the order of service does not consist of readings and a sermon of the sort with which I am familiar but rather is composed of a lively, often high-spirited discussion on various topics. I must confess, at first their gatherings looked more like a group of friends gabbing over coffee than the worship services familiar to me. But when I listened to the content of their discussions, I was inspired by the genuine faithfulness, the willingness to be vulnerable, and the spirit of mutual encouragement that filled those gatherings as they openly shared personal struggles.

At this point, I have been to SGI meetings of many types in many different countries. I have also been to some grand SGI centers in major cities, like London, Seoul, New York, Tokyo, and Singapore. The SGI certainly understands hospitality, and the members know how to put on a show. I have attended cultural festivals with thousands of performers, featuring beautiful dance performances, music, and feats of gymnastics. I have participated in large-scale general meetings both in the United States and in Japan, and seen them gather hundreds, and even thousands, of people to hear eloquent speeches filled with an air of solemnity. All of these have impressed me. But I have come to appreciate that, as impressive as their facilities may be, and as grand as many of the events I have attended were, the heart of the SGI is in small group discussion meetings held in local neighborhoods for people living in those communities. They do not have pipe organs and mass choirs to complement their chanting. In that respect they resemble Islam. Musical talent and soloists, however, are included in many other cultural programs.

In 1947, there were a handful of Soka Gakkai members struggling to rebuild their communities out of the wreckage of postwar Japan. Then as now, discussion meetings like the one the nineteen-year-old Daisaku Ikeda attended on August 14 of that year were the mainstay of the organization. Today they have millions of adherents worldwide—but they are still meeting in one another's homes.

How has the SGI grown so rapidly, from a small Japanese community of just a few thousand in 1951 to an organization of more than twelve million members in 192 nations and territories around the world today?

I understand from Ikeda that the discussion meeting has always been the heart and soul of the SGI organization, that this is the "home" for all SGI members, the place where almost every member (including Ikeda himself) first encountered Nichiren Buddhism. It has grown to an astonishing membership in large part because of these home gatherings.

I have come to appreciate that the SGI gatherings are full of both new introductions and constant affirmations. Their discussions are feasts of affirmative words, ideas, and possibilities. It seems to me that Ikeda has inspired a great discussion that is alive throughout the organization he worked so hard to build. I have seen these discussions take place in small gatherings in Atlanta, in Los Angeles, in Australia, in Africa, in New Zealand, in Singapore, and in many other places around the world; always they are lively and filled with inspiring ideas. The SGI is an organizational spiritual affirmatorium seeking to achieve everybody's enlightenment and happiness.

In Christianity, we do not always have a meaningful theological family meal on Sunday mornings. As rich and fulfilling as our faith and beliefs are, we as congregations do not actively participate in a communal feast of intellectual sharing, where we all enjoy a bounty of nourishment, where we all share our ideas, our education, and our experiences. Instead, too often, we sit in pews and listen to someone else profess our faith to us. Though we may clap and stand, cheer and sing and shout, we do not join our voices into a chorus of dialogue the way I have seen in the SGI. This chorus of shared openness of ideas is precisely the atmosphere I have tried to cultivate in my classroom and to create at the Martin Luther King Jr. International Chapel, especially in our sermon "talk-backs" following the worship services where the congregation is invited to become active participants in our theological dialogue about faith.

Our sacred Christian texts offer principles and guidance, but our texts need to live. We need to explore their application and meaning through reflection, discussion, criticism, and debate, striving to improve how faithfully we adhere to what Martin Luther King Jr. called making "a career of humanity."

Ikeda believes that the sacred texts of his faith tradition, the writings of Nichiren Daishonin and the Lotus Sutra, are the beginning, not the end, of all discussion. For him, those sacred texts are a springboard for debate and discussion—an opportunity to apply what they hold sacred to their lives in order to maintain their transformative relevance. Ikeda realizes that the teaching of those texts needs to be understood in a modern context, so he has produced other writings that interpret Nichiren tradition in light of contemporary issues. Because those teachings are timeless, he has worked to ensure that their message transcends time and space, speaking effectively and humanely to people today. Through Ikeda's work, and by his example, the Buddhists in the SGI have also been invited to engage in this reflection and discussion with equally serious intensity. Ikeda is striving toward a more perfect understanding of the teachings of Buddhism, but I do not think he believes that what he has to say on the subject is the final word. He expects his followers to continue in the path of unconditional understanding and truer application that he has modeled for them.

By the seriousness with which SGI Buddhists take their practice and study of faith, they have inspired me to lead the people with whom I minister to be just as reflective, serious, and engaged. Great spiritual traditions all possess excellent principles and ways of living, but they are often misunderstood because of the imperfections, literalisms, and excesses of their most public proponents. Many young people in America have become disenchanted with church because they genuinely feel wounded by the teachings and dismayed by the intolerance of judgmental versions of Christianity being offered to them. This is one reason the unnamed successors to the Millennials are being described as post-institutional.

For religion to play a vital and revitalizing role, for it to inspire people to be their better selves and work together for the common good, its principles need to be internalized, not just institutionalized. Our churches should be headlights toward the future, not taillights warning everyone to stay back. Instead of being seen as a set of rules that must be obeyed, religion should be seen as a source of invigorating faith and audacious hope, relevant decisions and dynamic action in moral situations that nurture and inspire us, helping us to become more self-actualized, moving into wholeness.

I believe this is what Ikeda strives toward—the humanization of religion and the internalization of its best principles. He strives toward a more perfect understanding of the traditions of his faith. More, he inspires all of us toward a more perfect understanding of our own beliefs, and to their more perfect application in the world. This is not a task that is ever completed. It is always a work in progress. Success is a moving target.

What I have learned powerfully over the years is that the professor may have the degree, may have mastered the subject matter, and may be more knowledgeable about the reading matter than the students, but a dialogical, question-and-answer approach permits the students to contribute valuable personal experiences and discoveries. This approach sets up a dynamic that motivates the different participants in the class to stretch and to grow—something that the professor alone could not do. When everybody can weigh in with some kind of critique, or simply with a question, you can almost witness the students transforming. I can witness myself growing. And that has made my classes dynamic and popular at Morehouse.

The SGI's congregational model of discussion meetings held in members' homes is the same model used by organized gatherings of believers in the first Christian churches throughout the Greco-Roman world. In those first decades and centuries after Jesus's resurrection and ascension, members of Christian communities met in people's homes. Families would gather and cheer one another. These gatherings were the place where pastoral care was expressed, and where the faithful met and prayed and studied together.

It was in these house gatherings that decisions were ultimately made to write the stories down that would become sources of the Gospel accounts of Jesus, since many of the eyewitnesses to Jesus were dying. So it is not surprising that the house gatherings of the followers of the Way, as the early church was called, collected stories from particular houses, and the collections took on the names of the Apostles around whom the believers gathered and heard tell of their recollections of Jesus's teachings.

The Gospels of Matthew, Mark, Luke, and John were not necessarily put to paper by the men for whom those works are named. Stories about these men, their times, and their views of Jesus's life and teachings were expressed and shared by the Apostles as eyewitnesses to history at house meetings. Gradually, communities grew around common interpretations, stories, traditions of worship and belief expressed by legends about Jesus that were told fragmentally. Later, as the people who witnessed what those men said and did were beginning to pass on, it became important to commit those stories to writing. The Gospels we have today are the fruits of the stories that came out of those community house churches that eventually stretched across Asia Minor and throughout the Greco-Roman world. Those early communities spread as quickly as the SGI and, I believe, for much the same reason—because of the powerful intimacy and encouragement of dialogue.

As Christianity developed and the institution of the Church grew more powerful and prominent, the early tradition of shared worship and discussion gave way to a canonization of Scripture and an installation of a priestly class who alone was authorized to preach the Word of the Lord. Today, there are few sermon talk-backs or dialogues with the preacher where the congregation is given equal time, and this demonstrates how much the dynamic, collaborative communalism of early Christianity has faded.

One of the tragic things about the black church is that the black pulpit provides a route to leadership and prominence in the black community too easily. Black people are a little superstitious, and when a person says, "I have been called to preach," something pops up in the black consciousness that becomes very respectful: "Touch not the Lord's anointed! Whatever this person says must be Gospel truth."

People are often ignorant of the supporting literature that is available to buttress faith. Too often access to that literature is confined to the seminaries. It does not trickle down. The pastor has a seminary education, but there is no mandate to share that knowledge with the congregation. For example, most pastors in the Christian church never teach any church history. They do not really even teach theology. They tell Bible stories, and they frequently do not tell them well, because they transport them across the centuries and drop them on people as imperatives. The congregation does not know the cultural context in which these Scriptures were created. They do not know who wrote them or what the issues were of the day. Pastors give these ancient texts authority over people's lives in a time very different from the time they were written. For instance, they treat the Bible as though there is a consistent sexual ethic in it—and there just is not. Pastors also make texts do work that their authors never intended for them to do. This is why a learned ministry is so important.

I have always believed that the Christian church would be a great deal stronger today had it maintained those house meetings where people were grappling with these texts and ideas together. There is more effective pastoral care expressed at an SGI meeting than in most Christian churches because the discussion is centered on sharing what is happening in one another's lives. The Christian church only knows you are there when there is a crisis, a loss, an emergency, or money is needed. Otherwise, you are part of the woodwork.

The Sunday school hour in a Christian church is often the greatest hour of the sharing and swapping of biblical and historical ignorance. In an adult class, there is always a lesson for that Sunday. They begin with the Scripture and people go around the room and give their opinions. And that is it. It does not reach the ideal of the Jewish Talmud, which is a collection of all of the different scriptural commentaries and informed opinions of the rabbis over the centuries. The Christian literature has not risen to that level. It has neither the depth of an SGI study group, nor the intimacy of an early Christian house meeting. It is just "What do you think?" That is where the swapping of ignorance comes in. Then class is over. Nobody knows Greek and Hebrew. They seldom really deal with the contextual meaning of words or the origins of those words or what they meant to the writers who used them, except maybe from the pulpit. We impose our contemporary meaning on them instead. And we do not bring anything with us to supplement the Bible, no works by contemporary writers that might help us to understand what we have read. That is why Sunday schools, and Christian education in general, are so weak. But an even bigger issue is that there is no dialogue with other religious traditions.

Yet the best solutions to the most pressing political and humanitarian crises of our times have come to us through cross-fertilization—ideas being communicated across time and cultures, enriched by different spiritual traditions, even building bridges among them. Even the American nonviolent Civil Rights Movement and the creation of the internet has international roots.

An Indian Hindu freedom fighter led a struggle to release his people from centuries of colonial rule. He inspired an African American Christian minister to lead the most ecumenical and transformative nonviolent social movement for human rights in US history. A Japanese Buddhist leader came to believe in his work and ideals through his own spiritual odyssey and has taken his ideals and made them part of his spiritual message to the world. And this Japanese Buddhist has established institutions to keep those ideals alive in the hearts of future generations.

Social activism has a rich history in many religious traditions. It abounds with wisdom from many great women and men. But if we do not think more creatively, we will never be aware of the abundance of this shared treasury of human wisdom. We all have our own silos that limit what we value, who we can become, and what we hear, see, smell, and touch. But to claim the best of human wisdom that is our shared human heritage, it is important to think beyond them. Learning to talk to one another, to share experiences and ideas, to ask one another questions, and to hear one another's stories—that is how we can begin to do this.

There is an African proverb from the Ganda tribe in Central Uganda that says, "He who never visits thinks his mother is the best cook." We must leave home spiritually to learn how to deal with the cultural diversity in the world. It's traveling time. Gandhi calls us to live in the "global village," King calls us to live in the world house, Ikeda calls us to live in the commonwealth of global citizens, and Mandela calls us to live in the "solidarity of peace-loving nations."

Any meaningful discussion of nonviolence has to talk about humanizing religious institutions. When I think of the history of global conflict, it disturbs me that religion is too often on the side of war and violence rather than being a beacon of sustainable peace.

My intention here is not to critique any specific religion, or to lump all religions into a single category. Rather, I want to critique exclusivist doctrines and violent extremism that wrap themselves in the mantle of religion and claim religious justification for their actions. My hope is to foster interreligious dialogue and to model a spirit of interfaith affirmative, sustainable cooperation. I want to learn from my siblings of different faiths. I believe all traditions are enriched being in discourse with one another, and I believe each one of us is enriched by a willingness to listen and to learn. We are moving toward a global culture of peace and nonviolence.

Religious fundamentalism and religious exclusivism are all, to me, signs that growth has stopped. When spiritual communities say, in essence, "I have nothing to learn from you" or "I am 100 percent sure that I am correct and 100 percent sure that you are wrong," these are indications that a community has lost sight of its responsibility to inspire mature growth and evolutionary emergence. It is a sign that a religion or a community has been infected by anti-intellectual violence and "ontological terror."

There are now more American Muslims than there are Episcopalians, Jews, and Presbyterians combined. Los Angeles is now the largest Buddhist city in the Western hemisphere. Chaplains of all faiths serve the American military. Religious diversity is as much a part of our national fabric as is our cultural, ethnic, and political diversity. Muslims are not only in the Middle East, Hindus are not all in India, and Buddhists are not all in Asia. Sikhs are becoming an increasingly visible segment of the American population. There are now six million Jews in Israel and five and a half million in America. We have the ability right where we are to foster interfaith cooperation and mutual learning.

In the ecumenism I have tried to foster in the Martin Luther King Jr. International Chapel, I have highlighted the nonviolent peace movements of Mahatma Gandhi, Martin Luther King Jr., Nelson Mandela, and Daisaku Ikeda—individuals who have shaped and led large mass movements based on principles that are profoundly related to one another. It is significant to me that these men come from different faith traditions and different cultures, and that they were responding to different historical conditions; yet all four shared a vision of global peace.

We must engage in a meaningful ethical pluralism: in terms of race and ethnicity, in terms of culture, and in terms of interreligious dialogue. We must, in the United States, celebrate the many peoples who have participated in the development of our nation—the indigenous peoples, the Protestant and Catholic settlers fleeing religious persecution, the immigrants from different parts of Europe, and the enslaved Africans forcibly brought here to make an essential contribution to building the wealth of this nation. We must also celebrate the Muslims and Hindus, the Buddhists and Mormons who (among so many others) are participating today in the ongoing story of our national evolutionary growth. We must celebrate that all of us together embody the highest fruits of wisdom from the entire treasury of human spirituality. We must celebrate this richness, with the spirit of "one river, many wells," and we must make this rich diversity work for us, *E pluribus unum*, "out of many, one" or "many uniting into one." We must tap the spiritual resources we have at hand and not close ourselves off because this or that idea does not come wrapped in a package we understand.

Booker T. Washington famously urged the integration and separatism of blacks and whites by saying, "Cast down your bucket where you are." These words are still true today—at a time of great spiritual crisis, we must cast down our buckets where we are and pull often from the well of human wisdom that resides in the United States but comes to us from all around the world.

I have faith that the many pressing issues facing our planet today—terrorism, environmental degradation, the rise of oppressive fundamentalism in many faith traditions, inequality between men and women the world over, the fact that white Americans with a college degree are on average three times as wealthy as black Americans with the same credentials, the fact that the top 1 percent of Americans control 40 percent of the nation's wealth, inequality in American democracy and the American system of justice, and lack of trust in American institutions[36]—will be resolved by committed, passionate, and wise young people, inspired by the best ideas from disparate and diverse cultural and religious traditions. Because I believe this, I want to answer Gandhi and King's call and join in the efforts of Daisaku Ikeda to create institutions dedicated to bringing ideas and people together, moral cosmopolitan dialogical citizens and friends.

Chapter Ten

Education for Cosmic Citizenship and Friendship

I have spent my entire career studying and teaching, and Daisaku Ikeda has said many times that he wants to crown his career with his contributions in the educational arena. For both of us, the work of education and teaching is our opportunity to work with young people and, in that way, to have a hand in creating the future. This is a sacred task, a calling, and a vocation in the most devout sense, and for both of us, I believe our faith has inspired a dedication to education.

I hold a PhD from Boston University, five honorary degrees, and have held academic appointments since finishing school, including thirty-nine years as dean of the chapel and professor of religion at Morehouse College. Ikeda is the founder of the Soka schools system, and two Soka universities, one in Japan and one in the United States.

Yet because of the challenges he faced, Ikeda completed only junior college, and although he holds nearly four hundred honorary degrees from universities around the world, he has not attended graduate school in any particular field. Nevertheless, Ikeda's erudition is impressive and his list of publications would be enviable to even the most productive academics. Clearly, Ikeda is a man of letters and learning, as seen in his numerous publications on Buddhism and on peace and nonviolence. He has published more than eighty dialogues with prominent figures from around the world in the humanities, politics, faith traditions, culture, education, and various academic fields. He has lectured at the most prestigious universities in the world.

It is my considered option that the broadness of his interdisciplinary education is a result of him having studied with this mentor, Josei Toda, for a complete decade. It is appropriate to say that this "Toda University" represents perhaps one of the greatest mentor-disciple relationships of the twentieth century.

If I experienced limitations as a young African American seeking an education in the United States before the Civil Rights Movement, Daisaku Ikeda's educational opportunities were also limited, in large part due to the militarization of the educational system in Japan. The education he received was not aimed at fostering the growth of learned and capable citizens but, rather, was designed to produce willing soldiers and loyal subjects to a military imperial regime. I believe that it was these experiences that lie at the heart of Ikeda's dedication to a type of education aimed at cultivating individuality, creativity, critical thinking, and cosmopolitan consciousness.

Ikeda grew up in poverty, lived with a life-threatening illness, and experienced firsthand the devastations of war.

I, too, was raised in difficult economic circumstances, as my mother reared me with the help of her sister, Eddie Kate Mays, and struggled to provide the kind of home she wanted for me. My entire first year of elementary school was spent at home with one childhood illness after another, including measles, mumps, chicken pox, and whooping cough. Dr. Houston informed my parents that I was close to death. I also grew up as an African American in the middle of the twentieth century, before the serious educational inequalities between black children and white children became a national concern and on the eve of the nonviolent Civil Rights Movement.

Although we grew up in two different worlds, Ikeda and I have a perspicacious kinship because we each climbed steep and arduous roads to earn our education and, as a result, have forged a strong commitment to this venture. We share a lifelong passion for education.

I grew up in Columbus, Ohio, home of The Ohio State University, the world's largest single campus university. But even though they won five national football championships in the years I lived there, I never went to a game or heard their world-renowned marching band. I lived within a few miles of the university, but in fifteen years I never once went to the stadium. Today this amazes me. I grew up in the shadow of this fine institution but never aspired to go there. In fact, I was discouraged from any such ambition and told that Ohio State was too difficult for someone like me. I was not smart enough for such a place.

Little was offered to me in the way of encouragement or inspiration educationally. No one told me that the walk I took to church four times a week, down the street where I lived, led past the house where Jesse Owens used to live. I did not know about this great African American man, not only an acclaimed athlete, but the courageous hero who exposed the lie of Nazi Germany's claims to Aryan racial supremacy at the 1936 Olympics. If I had known that Owens had grown up in my community, on my street, I would have thought more highly of it and been more proud of the place I was from. I might have known that the world was full of possibilities for me.

I grew up in a time when not much was expected of people of African descent. That is why I want the young people I teach to be exposed to great ideas, remarkable people, and notable, significant places. I want them to know what is possible for them to achieve. I express high expectations.

This is not to say that I had a deprived childhood; far from it. I describe the difficulties I experienced so that people will know that flowers can bloom even in inhospitable soil. My home was full of love and nurturing, which I was blessed to receive in abundance from the loving women who raised me and from some remarkable teachers I had in school. Without them, I would not be half the person I am today. All of my public school teachers from the fifth grade to the twelfth grade were white.

When I transferred from an all-black elementary school

to a nominally racially integrated school, I was one of a small number of African Americans in the entire building. One of my teachers, a white woman named Josephine Clark, would call on everyone to read in turn. When my turn came, I often missed words—sometimes I would mispronounce them, or if I did not know the word at all, I might skip it altogether. When I did this, the other students would laugh. So I laughed with them. What else could I have done? I had always preferred to pretend to be in on the joke, rather than being the butt of it.

After one class, Mrs. Clark asked me directly, "Would you like to learn how to read?"

I was thrilled by her question, and I told her excitedly that I would.

She said matter-of-factly, "Why not stay after class, and I will help you." She did not make a big deal of it, or act like she was doing me any special favor. She simply told me that I would have to work extra hard to improve my reading skills, and that she would help me do it. I was stunned, in fact amazed, that this white lady was willing to miss going home on time to be with her family in order to stay after school and help me, a little ignorant black boy, learn how to read. I was overcome with heavenly joy that the secrets to the science of reading were about to be unlocked and given to me! This was the true beginning of my scholarly career at the Highland Avenue Elementary School at 40 South Highland Avenue in Columbus, Ohio.

So that day I stayed after school and did so for many

afternoons over the following weeks. That remarkable woman taught me how to read properly. I now understand that she took time away from her lesson planning and grading, and even from her personal affairs, in order to help me. But she never made me feel like I was a backward little boy who needed help. I was a student, and she was my teacher.

Josephine Clark—I will never forget her. She was the first white teacher to take a personal interest in me, and by the effort she made, she let me know that she believed I was just as intelligent and able as the other children, and that she expected me to do the work to demonstrate that.

It is said that education is what remains after one has forgotten everything learned in school. I know this is true because of teachers like Mrs. Clark. Because I understand this, I take seriously the example I set for my students, and the way that I treat them.

Ikeda has written about teachers he had in elementary school who had a profound impact on shaping his character, not because of specific lessons about arithmetic or history they imparted, but because of what they taught him about life.

Ikeda insists that he was an unremarkable student in grade school and middle school. I suppose this may be true. Then again, I do not think young children really have a good basis to assess their own abilities or talents in relation to others. As children, were not we all merely concerned with making friends and earning the approval of the adults we loved? Was not it over time that we discovered what we were good at and where our talents lay? At that young age, all we really knew was what we enjoyed doing, and it usually was not clear to us until a little later that these might become useful skills. I know that at that age Ikeda loved reading and history, and so while he felt completely unremarkable as a student, I am quite sure his parents and his teachers saw an unusually curious and thoughtful young boy.

When Daisaku was eight years old, his class was taught by an energetic young man, newly minted and fresh out of teachers' college. I think students always have a special fondness for young and eager teachers, so it does not surprise me that this man would have made an impression on the young boy.

Ikeda recalls that at the end of each school day, the students took turns cleaning the classroom and were sent home only if their chores passed the teacher's muster. Sometimes, however, he would be so busy with his lessons or his grading that he would tell them he would check on their work later and just send the children home. Knowing how young children are in a hurry to run off, I suspect on many occasions, the teacher would have to tidy up after them; he probably felt his time was better spent doing his work than supervising the youngsters.

But Ikeda says that he understood that if his work was not up to snuff, the teacher would have to do it. When Daisaku knew his teacher was busy, he took extra care with the nightly chores. Instead of rushing off after being dismissed, the boy would check the cleaning of the room himself, often doing one of the chores again, just to make sure it was done correctly.

One day, as he was rinsing rags that had been used to wash the blackboard, his teacher walked in and noticed him working quietly alone. Without a word, he joined the boy at the bucket to rinse the rags. When Ikeda wrote about this moment years later, he said that in that simple gesture, not only did the teacher acknowledge his diligence, but he expressed his appreciation and did this without saying a single word.

At the same time, he taught the young boy a valuable lesson about knowing when it was time to play and when it was time to work.

When Ikeda tells that story today, he says this teacher taught him about character, about gratitude, and about valuing what others have done to support you. He also taught the boy lessons about generosity, about paying attention to what others are experiencing. In class, children can learn many things, but for a smart and bookish boy like Daisaku Ikeda, lessons could have been learned by reading on his own. But lessons in life and character can only be learned through face-to-face interaction with caring people.

Though Daisaku Ikeda and I grew up in different countries, under vastly different circumstances, we both understand that education has the power to crush a child's spirit or to elevate it.

But how I struggled with this. I felt a strong calling to become a minister, and yet sometimes, I doubted myself so much. I doubted what I had to offer, doubted why God would call someone as unworthy as me to preach His word. Today I understand that doubt was not given to me by God. It was not something innate. It was something I was taught to have, a feeling of being less than, for no reason other than the color of my skin. And I know that you cannot respond well to a Christian vocational call if you do not like yourself.

I understand what it means to grow up without opportunity, to feel some potential and value in myself, but not to see any opportunity to realize that potential. I know how important are the messages that we send our young people, how meaningful even the tiniest or most casual lesson can be.

What I remember most about my school days was the persistent feeling that I was inadequate as a student. Of course, this cannot have been entirely true. I did well in school, even compared to my white classmates. I was accepted into a private Baptist college, and I did well enough there to pursue graduate school at Boston University. That in itself should be enough evidence that I was not such a poor student.

But the fact remains that I did not feel academically equipped. Instead of discouraging me, however, that insecurity fueled in me a strong feeling that what I lacked in natural ability I had to make up for in hard work. And so, though self-doubt is not a good or healthy thing, it did motivate me to apply myself to my studies with serious dedication. I did not believe I was as smart or as talented as the white children around me. At the same time, I knew I had something to offer. This complicated mix of feelings followed me through my doctoral studies.

I went to Boston University because Martin Luther King Jr. and Otis A. Maxfield had gone there and because they were my heroes. They were my inspiration and my role models. Despite my feeling unworthy, their examples were important enough to me that I nevertheless undertook the daunting process of earning my doctorate. They gave me that faith in myself.

When I was a first-year graduate student at Boston University, I lived in a suite with three roommates at 745 Commonwealth Avenue on the fifth floor of the School of Theology. It was a two-bedroom suite, with a shared study area between the two bedrooms, and each of us had a desk in a different corner. My three roommates, all white, seemed to be well prepared for graduate study in theology and were speed-readers. I felt certain they were better prepared than I was. We were all admitted to the same program at the same school, and so in principle I was just as qualified as they were. But I felt deep inside that I was not as ready or as able as my fellow students.

My roommates all completed the program in three years. I took four. This was a deliberate choice on my part. I chose to extend my stay an additional year so that I could take fewer courses each term to allow myself more time to study.

I knew myself. I wanted to obtain additional degrees, so I decided to give myself the best chance to acquire strong grades. My roommates, on the other hand, had no such academic ambitions and planned to graduate and go on to pastor churches.

But those roommates became my friends and were a great support to me. I did not expect this. They saw me staying up later than anyone, staying home on weekends to read and prepare for class, and at some point, they started doing things to let me know that they were going to stand by me in my efforts to excel in school. It felt good to know that we were all in this struggle together. In a quiet but powerful way, we made an effort to be there for one another.

My first semester I had some trouble in my New Testament class, mostly because I found Professor Donald Rowlingson dull, monotone, and uninteresting, as did the majority of the large class. Unfortunately, by the time finals rolled around, I was in a difficult spot. I was not prepared for the final exam and was worried. This was the one class where I felt my performance would not be up to par.

On the night before the final, I stayed up all night to study. I was frustrated and discouraged and, frankly, emotionally overwrought. One of my roommates, Richard Lee Weber, a United Methodist from Pittsburgh, Pennsylvania, (who was later the best man at my wedding in Waco, Texas, and I at his), saw that I was struggling and decided, for some mysterious reason, that he needed that very night to wash and iron every stitch of clothing he owned. He stayed awake with me in the common room the entire night. Richard never explained what he was doing, but I understood. In the middle of the long and difficult night, it helped to have someone else in the room with me. We did not talk, but I knew he was there, and I knew that he wanted me to do well on my final exam. Over the years my confidence improved, and so did my grades.

I consider Daisaku Ikeda's efforts to inspire young people as perhaps the signal accomplishment of his life. I am struck by how often he says that he regards himself as an educator and that education is his life's work. Education, for Ikeda, is not simply about imparting knowledge. Global citizenship depends on devoting ourselves to education.

During my acquaintance with the SGI, I have had the opportunity to meet many of their young people and am always impressed by their genuine commitment to interpersonal nonviolent social change. Without exception, they have told me their commitment was inspired by Daisaku Ikeda.

I remember the old slogan of the United Negro College Fund, "A mind is a terrible thing to waste, but a wonderful thing to invest in." I believe that. A child comes into the world with great curiosity, and we must do everything we can to patiently nurture the creativity and to encourage the curiosity of all children.

Chapter Eleven

Value Creation

As you drive through the charming and crowded town of Hachioji, an hour outside of Tokyo, you approach the main entrance to Soka University. Founded by Daisaku Ikeda in 1971, it has become recognized in just under five decades as a leading university in Japan. As you enter the university, you see a beautiful stone calligraphy of the Japanese characters for *Soka Daigaku*, or Soka University, cast from the handwriting of Tsunesaburo Makiguchi, the person who developed the principles of Soka pedagogy and was the founder and first president of the Soka Gakkai.

Makiguchi was a reformist educator, geographer, philosopher, and author who at the beginning of the twentieth century sought to understand pedagogy in a way that was different from the traditional Japanese perspective. Japanese education, especially during the Meiji era, was focused on making children the loyal subjects of the emperor and good workers for the state. In both content and practice, classroom instruction emphasized obedience to authority, respect for tradition, and rote mastery of established ideas.

In contrast, Makiguchi believed that education should

foster creative individuals whose purpose in life was what we might now call self-actualization—the fullest development of their own character and ability.

Makiguchi was influenced by western philosophers such as Jean-Jacques Rousseau, Immanuel Kant, and the American educational reformer John Dewey. He gathered other like-minded educators of his day to discuss his ideas, and in his search to find the best means for developing an individual's innate potential, he was unexpectedly led to the teachings of Buddhism—and specifically the teachings of Nichiren.

Japanese Buddhism at that time did not see itself as a teaching of self-actualization or empowerment. Despite the centuries-long tradition of Buddhist rituals and worship, the actual study of the Buddha's teachings was not common. In many ways the place of Buddhism in Japan was not unlike that of Christianity in America today, where few people actually understand the scope and context of the teachings of Jesus. Buddhism's role in Japanese society had become largely ceremonial and ritualistic. Though the Buddha's teachings had a profound impact on Japanese thought and culture, a practical application of Buddhist principles was not particularly widespread.

Nichiren was a thirteenth-century Buddhist teacher and innovator who first taught the practice of venerating the Lotus Sutra. He promoted the practice of reciting Nam-myoho-renge-kyo, the Japanese rendering of the title of that sutra, as a way of manifesting each person's innate Buddha potential. When Makiguchi encountered Nichiren's writings, he was astonished to learn that Nichiren Buddhism was first and foremost a practice by which all people could develop their own unique abilities. And as he began his own practice of Nichiren's teachings, he felt he had found the spiritual underpinning for his own thinking about education.

Makiguchi had already developed a strong pedagogical basis for his approach to teaching over the course of his career, but now Buddhism added a philosophical depth to his theory. In Nichiren's writings he found a concrete practice through which anyone could attain enlightenment, which Makiguchi interpreted in secular terms as manifesting one's highest potential. Makiguchi believed this should also be the ultimate goal of education.

Makiguchi's masterwork—*The System of Value-Creating Pedagogy*—took years of his life to write. It outlines the range of thinking he had done on this subject over the course of many decades. In his book, he argues that the purpose of life was "value creation," which was, for him, the highest form of creativity. But creativity, as Makiguchi understood it, did not simply refer to the ability to create art or music. He noted that one of the things that distinguished human beings from other animals was our ability to learn, to innovate, and to create. Human history has always advanced through a process of creative problem solving.

For Makiguchi, creativity was the innate potential within each of us to create meaning and value from the materials of our lives and circumstances. Cultivating this highest form of creativity was, for Makiguchi, the aim of education. He believed that the purpose of life was for each person to become happy, but not in the nihilistic sense of seeking only pleasure or momentary satisfaction. Happiness for Makiguchi was rooted in creating good out of the challenges and difficulties that people face in their lives. Creating good referred to the development of their individual character, but it also referred to their actions on behalf of social good, contributing to the betterment of society. An ethic of mutual value creation, where all people could create their own individual satisfaction while contributing to the betterment of society, was the purpose of Makiguchi's pedagogy, and the phrase "value creation," *or soka*, became the name of the Buddhist community he founded.

Makiguchi's ideas for educational reform were controversial in pre-World War II Japan. In fact, his trenchant critique of Japanese education was viewed with great suspicion by Japan's militaristic regime.

Makiguchi imagined that one day the principles he was working out would become expressed in a transformative educational system, encompassing primary and secondary education and culminating in a university that would embody his educational aims. When Soka University was opened in Hachioji in 1971 by Daisaku Ikeda, decades after Makiguchi's death in prison, it was the highest institutional expression of Makiguchi's educational system.

Higher education in Japan was generally reserved for the

privileged, and admission into a top-flight university guaranteed access to the positions of greatest power and prestige in Japanese society. Education, especially university education, was not viewed as having the goal of providing opportunity for talented students from any social station to cultivate their abilities. Rather, it was a vehicle to perpetuate distinctions in class and privilege. A university based on his theory of value creation was therefore crucial to Makiguchi's radical and democratic vision, a system of education that would enable all students, regardless of their background, to cultivate their abilities and create value in their lives and in society.

Makiguchi's ideas, though controversial, were well received among many educational theorists of his day. And Makiguchi's small group of followers was beginning to expand among other teachers, who agreed with Makiguchi's critique of Japanese education and were dedicated to its reform. As Makiguchi's commitment to Buddhism deepened, however, his group of educators gradually broadened their focus to encompass religious propagation as well. They regarded his pedagogical treatise, *The System of Value-Creating Pedagogy*, as a significant contribution that could not only reform education but also rescue Japanese society from the disastrous imperialist course upon which the country was then embarking. The date of the text's publication, November 18, 1930, is now regarded as the date of the establishment of the Soka Kyoiku Gakkai, the precursor to today's Soka Gakkai. Gakkai means "society" or association, Soka Kyoiku means "value-creating education."

Unfortunately, their efforts in the realm of education and religion flew in the face of what was happening in Japanese society at the same time. Those years when Makiguchi began practicing and teaching Nichiren Buddhism, the years when he was developing his value-creating pedagogy, were also the years when the Japanese military government was pursuing conquest abroad and the solidification of national unity at home. Makiguchi's ideas on value creation, and the Buddhist ideals he began to espouse, could not have been more contrary to the direction his nation was moving.

As Japan headed down its militaristic road abroad, it became more repressive at home. In 1925, the Public Security Preservation Law was passed. When written, it was intended to suppress socialism and communism, but within a few years the law was being used to criminalize any political opposition. Then, in 1941, the Security Preservation Law was amended to formally include religious groups as targets of prosecution. The Japanese government formed a "thought police" to monitor publications and public discussions deemed as critical of the government, and "thought prosecutors" were appointed to either punish people deemed criminals or to "convert" them through forced "reeducation." Between 1925 and 1945, more than seventy thousand people were arrested under provisions of the Public Security Preservation Law.

In 1943 Makiguchi and Toda were arrested, along with other leaders of the Soka Kyoiku Gakkai. By this time, it had grown to about three thousand members. Though still largely a body of educators, it had come to accept members from different occupational backgrounds, including many urban poor. All of the association's leaders were offered the opportunity to recant their Nichiren Buddhist faith and adopt Shintoism, the official religion of the state. If they agreed to renounce their criticism of the Japanese government, of the Shinto religion, and of the war, they would be released from detention and pardoned from prosecution.

All of the arrested leaders, with the exception of Makiguchi and Toda, accepted these terms. Makiguchi and Toda were formally charged with denying the divinity of the emperor, lèse-majesté. With Makiguchi and Toda imprisoned, and with the rest of the leadership renouncing their faith, the Soka Kyoiku Gakkai fell apart.

On November 18, 1944, when he was seventy-three, Tsunesaburo Makiguchi died in the infirmary of the Tokyo Detention House in Sugamo, known commonly as Sugamo Prison. He had been held for nearly sixteen months. Though charged with blasphemy against the emperor, he was never tried or found guilty of any crime. He was a martyr to his beliefs.

Makiguchi fought unjust government censure until the last moment of his life to protect Nichiren Buddhism. He endured unspeakable atrocities—brutal interrogations, repeated torture, deprivations, and humiliating treatment that ignored the most basic human dignity. Not once did he compromise or waver in his commitment. In fact, he used prison as an opportunity to teach value creation and spread the teachings of Nichiren Buddhism, often engaging his interrogators in debate on these issues.

Josei Toda, peace activist, teacher, second president and architect of the Soka Gakkai, was released in July 1945, just weeks before the end of the war. Toda had been a successful entrepreneur, but his businesses were lost during the war. As the war was approaching its end, and the nation descending into turmoil, Toda set out to rebuild his life. But more importantly, he wanted to rebuild the religious organization he had worked with his mentor to build.

Though it had damaged his health, Toda's experience of arrest and imprisonment had not weakened his sense of religious commitment. Instead, while in prison, he achieved a profound spiritual epiphany, which inspired him to an even higher level of personal mission and commitment. In light of what he had been through, and to honor Makiguchi's martyrdom, Toda felt that it would not be enough merely to rebuild what had been lost.

Vast, revolutionary concepts unfolded in Toda's mind. First, the old name had to go. Soka Kyoiku Gakkai (Value-Creating Education Society) was too limited for the coming era. The activities of the organization could no longer be confined to the educational world; they must encompass politics, economics, culture, and every other phase of society, inspiring people with drive and hope, based on the eternal, unchanging philosophy of Nichiren Buddhism.

Toda decided to use core elements of the former organization to build an entirely new Soka Gakkai, one true to the spiritual beliefs of Makiguchi but with a more finely honed purpose.

The organization Makiguchi founded was initially a group of educators studying ideas for reforming the educational system. Toda understood that, as Makiguchi's understanding of Nichiren Buddhism grew, the pedagogical society he formed had become a religious organization. Amidst the rubble of postwar Japanese reconstruction, Toda saw that the organization needed to embrace its religious orientation. He was certain that the Buddhist principles espoused within the Soka Gakkai would not merely inspire people in their efforts to rebuild a just, prosperous, and peaceful society. He felt it could provide the spiritual basis for a better society—and a better world.

Still, Toda understood Makiguchi's long-range hopes and the wisdom of his educational vision. For the rest of his life, he held onto Makiguchi's dream for a Soka University, viewing it as a legacy that he was to inherit and the work he was to complete.

Josei Toda accomplished many remarkable things during his life, perhaps most notably, the reconstruction of the Soka Gakkai after World War II and laying the foundation for it to become a major religious movement in Japan. But I suspect that, for him, even this feat was simply a prelude to fulfilling a dream sacred to his teacher's heart. I find it moving that to the end of his days, Toda cherished in his heart the goal of someday building a Soka University.

Toda always intended that the Soka Gakkai would have an impact beyond the realm of religion. Propagating his faith was important to him, but it was important because he believed that in the social tumult of postwar Japan, what people needed most of all was integrity of character, rooted in spirituality. Upon this foundation, he believed that a truly democratic and peaceful nation could be built. So Toda's primary focus during the final years of his life was in the realm of spirituality and religion.

Since Japan did not have a historical tradition of democracy, Toda was concerned that democracy thrive in his nation. Toda hoped that his religious organization would be a force for cultivating intelligent, empowered, and peace-loving people among the Japanese populace, citizens who would be truly capable of democratic self-governance.

Toda passed away in 1958 without being able to turn his attention back to the realm of education. But he accomplished the rebuilding of the Soka Gakkai. And he passed his vision for what he hoped to accomplish to his disciple, Daisaku Ikeda, whom he mentored for ten years. Ikeda describes his mentorship by Toda as the defining experience of his life and the source of everything he has done and become.

Thirteen years later, in 1971, Ikeda formally opened Soka University. And he had the calligraphy of the words Soka University in Makiguchi's hand carved in stone to grace the entryway of the university. For me, that calligraphy represents a fulfillment of a vision passed from Makiguchi to Toda to Ikeda. When I saw Soka University for the first time, John Edward Masefield's eloquent words in praise of English universities came to mind: "There are few earthly things more beautiful than a university. It is a place where those who hate ignorance may strive to know, where those who perceive truth may strive to make others see."

Ikeda has inherited the legacy of Soka education, and this is the type of education to which he has dedicated his life. Soka education is at the heart of Ikeda's mission to create a culture of peace based on cosmopolitan ethics and an ethic of global and cosmic citizenship and friendship. The mission of Soka education is essentially the same as Martin Luther King Jr.'s vision to build the beloved community. It provides us with an alternative vision of our cosmic future—of our interdependence, of our diversity, of our stewardship of creation, of justice, of nonviolence, which transforms the victim and the perpetrator, and of personal and communal dignity.

Applying nonviolent principles and creating a culture of peace are not tasks for the faint of heart. This is why I believe a cosmopolitan system of ethical principles and moral education committed to fostering not only a theoretical understanding of nonviolence but a deeply rooted and practically minded commitment to it is essential in the world today. And this, in a general sense, is what I see as the significance of the educational institutions that Ikeda has founded based upon the ideals to which he has dedicated his life.

In 2001, Soka University of America was officially opened in Aliso Viejo, California. The highest honor of my life was being asked by the first president of the university, Daniel Y. Habuki, on behalf of Ikeda to deliver the dedication address on May 4, 2001. I titled my address "Growing Up Into Democracy's Crown," which is now posted on their website. This university shares the same name as her older sister institution, and the two schools are connected, both formally and informally. But Soka University of America is a decidedly unique venture, distinct from Soka University in Japan. It is a liberal arts college and a graduate university with its own two separate curricula emphases; its master's program in Educational Leadership and Societal Change graduated its first class in 2016; but even more, this school represents a significant part of Ikeda's institutional legacy.

Both the original Soka University of Japan and Soka University of America seek to offer a high quality undergraduate education that is on par with the best schools in both nations, and neither school is radically different from the finest schools of either country. The younger American university was rated among the top fifty liberal arts colleges in the country within twelve years of admitting its first class. Additionally, it has ranked third in the United States, after Princeton University and Rockefeller University, in terms of the ratio of endowment dollars per student. As the founder, Ikeda set the university principles of the Orange County, California, campus to:

Foster leaders of culture in the community,
Foster leaders of humanism in society,
Foster leaders of pacifism in the world,
Foster leaders for the creative coexistence of nature
and humanity.

Ikeda set the value orientation of SUA:

Soka University is founded upon the Buddhist principles of peace, human rights, and the sanctity of life. The curriculum is nonsectarian. Educational objectives are fostered at the university through the commitment to rigorous academic endeavors, free and open dialogue, and an appreciation for human diversity. Education is an integrating process in which students gain an awareness of the interdependence of themselves, others, and the environment. Wisdom, courage, and compassion—values treasured by the university—do not exist in isolation. They emerge in individuals as they learn the importance of service to others, to the natural world around them, and to the great cause of peace and freedom.

Ikeda set SUA's mottoes as:

Be philosophers of a renaissance of life.
Be world citizens in solidarity for peace.
Be the pioneers of a global civilization.

Ikeda set the mission of SUA as,

To foster a steady stream of global citizens committed to living a contributive life.

Makiguchi's original pedagogical proposals were rooted in a specific historical context, and he sought to give students an education that was relevant to their circumstances. His emphasis on imparting specific skills were what we now think of as experiential education, education by doing as much as by reading, reciting, or memorizing. But more importantly, the aim of his proposals was to equip students to create value in the context of their daily lives. In practical terms, his specific curricular proposals involved students spending a significant part of their school day in a work environment.

Makiguchi wanted to make education relevant to the lives of individual students. This is why he emphasized a type of learning and a class schedule that would take students out of the classroom and into the communities where they lived, equipping them practically to tackle the challenges they would face.

From the beginning, when the women and men charged with the task of building Soka University of America sat down together, their goal was to give students a first-rate education. With that in mind, they felt that the school's mission should be to prepare its students to become leaders in peace, human rights, environmental work, and in sustainable and equitable economic development.

Education has a basic function to give students the tools for their own economic self-sufficiency and well-being, and in that sense, to help them work toward the value of gain, which along with beauty and good are the three values of Soka. But if the highest of the values in Makiguchi's hierarchy is the value of good—an active commitment to making a better society—then students should be challenged to grapple seriously with the most important and most intractable issues facing our world. Students should study various subjects, such as literature, politics, economics, mathematics, science, philosophy, ethics, and religion. But they should use those studies to understand the context of contemporary global conflicts and the human dimensions of the political and social fault lines that divide our world.

When I consider Soka University of America and its curricular emphases of fostering a steady stream of global citizens committed to living a contributive life, I feel that what Ikeda has done is to make the principles of Soka education that were first outlined by Tsunesaburo Makiguchi applicable to the global and social conflict issues in need of resolution that we face in the twenty-first century.

Tsunesaburo Makiguchi started as an educator, and in the process of developing a pedagogical system focused on fostering the best in young people, he encountered and embraced Nichiren Buddhism. His disciple, Josei Toda, was an educator who built on the work of Makiguchi but spent the last years of his life as a person of religion, establishing the Soka Gakkai as one of the largest religious communities in Japan. Toda's disciple, Ikeda, began his career focusing on religious endeavors but is now focusing on educational ones. In this way, the work of the first three presidents of the Soka Gakkai has come full circle. The ideal of value creation has its start and its end in the realm of education.

When I was approached to become a part of Soka University of America as a member of its board of trustees, I took the request seriously because the school's aims fit into the most important things I have hoped to accomplish in my career—to perpetuate and institutionalize the work for which Martin Luther King Jr. gave his life. I have not been disappointed. This experience has so far been very meaningful, and even pleasurable. I have been honored to be a part of launching a school that has set for itself the lofty ambition of graduating informed and aware global citizens and peace ambassadors.

There are, of course, good reasons why people question the founding of institutions of higher education by religious organizations. It is common in the United States today to view the work of liberal education as incompatible with the work of religion. In the so-called culture wars taking place in America today, there is a sense that religion has no place in the educational enterprise. On one side of the argument, people suggest that free inquiry and critical thinking are stifled by religious dogmatism. On the other, people of faith have expressed the feeling that many educational institutions are hostile to faith and belief. One side worries that the free and critical inquiry, the hallmark of the finest scholarship, is incompatible with the rigorous doctrinal beliefs held by people of strong faith. The other side worries that science and education have become hostile to faith and that young people who seek a quality higher education are asked to give up the beliefs they have inherited from their families.

One place where this debate is most critical is the battleground between Biblical Creation and the science of evolution. The story of Creation told in the Book of Genesis is seen by many as a myth that is unsupported, or even disproven, by science. Some people of faith suggest that the teaching of "intelligent design," the idea that the creation of the universe and the evolution of life on Earth were guided by some sort of divine intelligence, is a necessary corrective to ideas that would deny any sense of the spiritual or the divine within the workings of nature. As a result, in many schools around the country, the view of Creation held to be true by most of my Christian contemporaries is sometimes taught as a scientific theory or perspective, on a par with scientific views of evolution. Some view this as healthy, while others view it as an assault on reason, logic, and science.

I think that casting the debate in this way creates a false opposition between faith and reason. To me, Creationism—the belief that a Supreme Being is the author of heaven and earth rather than evolution—is essentially a matter of faith, and faith necessarily asks us to develop our understanding of things we cannot see or know. But faith also asks us to humbly refuse limitations on the Infinite, and to "love the Lord thy God with all thy heart, and with all thy soul, and with all thy *mind*"[37] (emphasis mine).

In contrast, education and science seek to understand and explain the physical world. I do not think the two perspectives are incompatible. As a person of faith, I can choose to believe in a vast and powerful divine intelligence, a theological ultimate, and I am not threatened in the least by learning the many fascinating facts about our physical world and how life has evolved over millennia. I believe that God created and sustains all diversity but that God is not diverse, but a unity. Education cannot teach faith, and at the same time, it cannot deny it. At the same time, I do not think that a faith can properly expect its believers not to think or reason, or ask them not to use their God-given intellect to its fullest.

Some people use faith as an excuse to stifle perspectives different from their own and regard questioning and critical thinking as opening a door to dangerous heresy. But this is not faith the way I practice or preach it, and I do not believe that the greatest spiritual teachers in human history have ever felt so insecure in their beliefs that they have had to suppress ideas that differed from their own.

The artificial opposition between faith and reason that I see raging around me ignores the historical fact that the great Western scholastic tradition was informed by great spiritual convictions, and that many of the finest institutions of higher education in the United States and Europe were founded first as seminaries or schools of theology. Morehouse College was founded by William Jefferson White, commissioned by the Washington National Theological

Institute and University. His intention was to educate young African American men to be ministers and teachers. Morehouse wanted to provide opportunity to people who had been denied it, considered less than human beings, and to give them the tools to improve their lives as well as their society.

So I have never seen education and religion as being inherently incompatible. I believe that a person of genuine faith can feel free to explore any question with an honest and open mind without fear. This is also Ikeda's view. We need to reframe the relationship between faith and education, and faith and science, not as an opposition between belief on the one hand and free inquiry on the other but as fundamentally distinct enterprises that can, and traditionally have, worked in concert in different aspects of people's lives.

In their highest purposes, education and faith have the same aim—to expand human consciousness and to make us greater, both individually and collectively, than we have been. Education is supposed to engage us in an evolutionary emergence, an expanding consciousness that allows us to overcome all impediments and relate fully with everything we encounter—all learning, all cultures. Education cannot answer all of our questions, and I do not think it is supposed to. But education does help us find the most meaningful questions to ask. Education is supposed to expand our lives and enlarge our addresses.

I practice my religion not only because I am commanded to but because I choose to. I choose to embrace my faith because I know that it affirms and elevates me, and brings me into alignment with the ultimate divine source. In a more general sense, I believe that the purpose of religion in human terms is to help us all express and develop to our fullest potential. In its best and truest sense, religion seeks the elevation of the human being toward a cooperative, creative awareness of the working of the cosmic law, the infinite intelligence in our lives and beyond.

Robert Browning says, "A man's reach must exceed his grasp, / Or what's a heaven for?" For me, the poet is suggesting that religion has taught us to aspire to something more, to motivate us all to become better. Education, too, has this goal. If we are inspired in this quest by religion, we are practically aided in its endeavor by education.

I consider the current ideological climate that creates the artificial opposition between deep spiritual faith and free and open inquiry to be bankrupt. This framework will not help us at all, and I do not want to deepen that particular divide. Instead, I want to see how faith and knowledge, belief and questioning, spiritual growth and scientific advancement can all support our individual betterment and improve the state of the world.

Because of this commitment, I have felt a strong affinity with the mission of Soka University of America ever since I learned of its values and goals. This school does not seek to be a Buddhist university and instead seeks teachers and students from a variety of faith (and nonfaith) traditions. But it is not ashamed of its origins in Buddhist philosophy. It does not teach Buddhist faith or practice, but it does embrace Buddhist values of peace, respect for the sanctity of life, and our harmonious coexistence with nature. These are certainly Christian values as much as Buddhist. And I know Muslims, Jews, and Hindus who share a commitment to these same values that are buttressed by their own faith traditions.

The SGI helped me understand that if Morehouse College was going to remain a flagship school in the twenty-first century, as it was in the twentieth, it had to be prepared to jump newer and higher hurdles. In the twentieth century the issue was civil rights and ending segregation. Morehouse was in the forefront of producing the leaders that brought about that change. Now the issues that confront us as a nation have more to do with difference, diversity, pluralism, terrorism, nuclear weapons, global warming, gun violence, unbridled capitalism, global conflict resolution, uses of technology, and health care. Morehouse cannot settle for the pristine glory of the past. That would be a violation of the statue of Martin Luther King Jr. that stands in front of the chapel as a reminder of what it means to be a Morehouse Man.

Ikeda has been called to actualize the dreams of Makiguchi and Toda, his mentor. This calling is not simply the desire to live a life dedicated to great ideals. It is a responsibility to give speeches and author documents and build institutions that will serve as a road map to future generations so they, too, can heed the call of value creation. Ikeda's vocation is not about what he can do; rather, it is about what he can leave behind so that his mentors' ideas continue to be taught and discussed—and realized cosmically.

Through my associations with Daisaku Ikeda and the SGI, I was beginning to understand, too, that King's vision of the world house also depended on education and the human revolution it offered. In this conviction I am echoing Thomas Jefferson, who wrote, "If a nation expects to be ignorant and free, in a state of civilisation, it expects what never was and never will be."[38]

Daisaku Ikeda is a faith mentor who has founded a kindergarten through twelfth grade educational system in Japan; kindergartens in Singapore, Hong Kong, Malaysia, and South Korea, a kindergarten and elementary school in Brazil; and two universities, one in Japan, one in America. All of these schools are built on a pedagogy of peace that seeks to inspire in students an ethic of service and accomplishment based not on competition but on cooperation. Like Makiguchi, Ikeda believes that where there is competition it should be compassionate competition. And at these schools, as the founder, he calls on his students to face head-on the real challenges of the world and overcome them using the tools of persuasion and dialogue, informed by the spirit of ahimsa and dedicated to the task of nonviolent social transformation. In this way, Ikeda has begun the work of institutionalizing the nonviolent philosophies of Mohandas K. Gandhi and of Martin Luther King Jr.

At both Soka University of America and Morehouse

College, we talk about fostering global leaders. We truly expect that our students will assume positions of leadership and servanthood and will exert themselves to address pressing global problems. At both institutions we need to be clear that our expectation of leadership from our students includes the requirement that they will possess qualities for cosmopolitan service, of unconditional love, and of faithful dedication to all. And this clarity of purpose will, I hope, assist us in educating excellent faithful servant scholars who embody the spirit of altruism. I hope that at both schools we can live up to the commitment to education and activism shared by Mahatma Gandhi, Martin Luther King Jr., Nelson Mandela, and Daisaku Ikeda.

Chapter Twelve

Global Commonwealth of Realized Citizens

Daisaku Ikeda's work as an educator and a builder of institutions is finally only the visible expression of an even more enduring legacy. In founding Soka University of Japan and America, spreading the SGI peace ambassadors around the world, Ikeda has also sought to modernize and humanize religion itself, while working to create a global commonwealth of dialogical citizens and friends.

With the Soka Gakkai International, Ikeda has brought a tradition rooted in millennia of Buddhist thought to bear upon problems facing our contemporary world; he has taken long-standing rituals and practices of Buddhism, distilled their spiritual essence, and made them relevant to people living today in cultures with no tradition of Buddhist thought or practice. But most of all, he has sought to use Buddhist teachings to call people, Buddhist and non-Buddhist alike, to seek the spiritual sources of their own traditions and to live in more fully human and more fully humane ways in the world.

I have studied Christian theology and have become

well acquainted with Hindu, Muslim, Jewish, and Buddhist principles of the divine. What is beautiful to see is the common feeling of reverence in all of these traditions toward whatever infinite force is at work in our lives, and that aspiration to live in the image and presence of what we perceive as eternal, transcendent, and ultimate.

In numerous faith traditions, this reverence—perhaps we can call it worship—can be seen as a kind of submission, and in most of our spiritual cultures, this is experienced as a surrendering of ourselves to the eternal divine or an ultimate sense of the sacred. However, I do not believe that such submission means to subjugate the human spirit; the infinite never seeks to deny or denigrate, block or limit the human soul.

All great spiritual traditions have at their core a set of teachings and principles with the ultimate aim of exalting the human spirit, elevating our spirit, and revealing what is best within each of us—in Christian terms, to find the qualities of God within each of us. More than helping individual humans to become better, I believe the truest and best purpose of religion is to help humanity as a whole become better. This is why Jesus spoke more about the kingdom than anything else.

I aim to make one simple point: the submission to divinity is the elevation of humanity.

In this sense, the highest expressions of spirituality, in whatever faith tradition one follows, are about truly humane affirmative, sustainable cooperation. We can quibble over the definition of "humanism," but for me, when a spiritual tradition seeks the elevation of the human spirit toward the divine, it is an expression of a fundamentally humanistic principle, and the most universal valuing of what it means to be a human being.

At the same time, as a Christian minister, I am struck by the discordance between what is most beautiful about the doctrines of my faith and how some people perceive it. It grieves me when people see Christianity as a force to oppress people, to exclude people, to condemn them, and force them into obedience with a lifestyle or a worldview that they may not share. I know the teachings of Jesus, and this is neither what he taught nor what he intended.

As a professor of religious studies, I am saddened that so much violent conflict in human history has been waged in the name of religion—that even today, people of religion, wearing the mantles of their faith, invoke, incite, and sometimes even instigate acts of violence. At the very least, they often create a climate for it. I cannot see how this is love or forgiveness in action. It certainly is not about peace.

That is why, when I was first introduced to the work of Daisaku Ikeda, I was impressed by his international grass-roots initiative of interfaith, interracial, and interdisciplinary discourse and cooperation. He has made significant contributions to help alleviate the problems of religious fundamentalism in the world.

All institutions aimed at human betterment—educational institutions and religious organizations chief among them—need to be humane, but the unfortunate truth is that too often many of our institutions formed with the aim of being "for the people" end up expecting people to serve the institution. These institutions, at their worst, are dehumanizing, even while they claim to be working for the good of the people.

In a speech Ikeda gave at Harvard University in 1991, he discussed the "organizational ossification" of religious institutions and described it as an all too common occurrence.

As religious convictions evolve into religious movements, organizational demands emerge. In my view, these institutional aspects of religions must constantly adapt to the changing conditions of society. Furthermore, they should support and give primary consideration to the personal, individual aspects of belief. The unfortunate truth, however, is that few religious movements have been able to avoid the pitfall of organizational ossification. The development of a religion's institutional features ends up shackling and restraining the people whose interests it originally intended to serve. The external coercive powers of ecclesiastical institutions and associated ritual stifle the internal and spontaneous powers of faith, and the original purity of faith is lost. Because this is such a common occurrence, we tend to forget that it actually represents a reversal of the true function of religion.[39]

Ikeda points out an interesting paradox of organized religion. Formed as communities to help people aspire toward the divine, they often end up stifling "the internal and spontaneous powers of faith." What Ikeda suggests is that instead of fostering love and a desire to seek mutual understanding even among so-called enemies, religious institutions become more interested in maintaining their own set of dogmatic rules and rituals. They become guardians of ecclesiastical authority and tradition, and this often devolves into intolerance and violence.

It is easy to cast blame on the institutions, but if it is organizational ossification that is part of the problem, then the solution must come from personal, individual reformation and rejuvenation. Religious institutions are constituted of individual people, and often we ourselves are complicit in their dysfunction. It is the personal responsibility of each one of us to recognize the rights of others. Each of us, individually, is responsible for humanizing the spheres of our own endeavors. Instead of wishing for change outside, we must, to reference Gandhi once again, "be the change we wish to see." Or, as Ikeda put it: "Only human will and action can create history and open new horizons"[40] and the power of our imagination allows us to "discover entranceways for exchange in the massive walls that divide our world."[41]

Ikeda's nonviolent humanism asserts that the awakening of the power of each person's potential through conscious evolution, aided by changes in cosmic consciousness itself, will lead to the realization of our potential as a social movement.

"A great human revolution in just a single individual will help achieve a change in the destiny of a nation,"[42] writes Ikeda. This belief in the social impact of a spiritually based self-mastery lies at the heart of his nonviolent philosophy.

Ikeda is also suspicious of systems of government and structures of power—the market economy, state authority—because of their tendency to make as their ultimate aim their own self-perpetuation. He is distrustful of institutions that seek to use human beings as a means to achieve their own profit or maintain their own power.

But although Ikeda's nonviolent humanism emphasizes the individual, it does not stop with personal conversion. Like Martin Luther King Jr., he understands that while social change starts with changing the hearts and minds of the individual, it is accomplished by acting through social structures.

Implicit in this view is the essential harmony of personal and political life. Compassion, cooperation, collaboration, and forgiveness are virtues that can and should be applied to politics, diplomacy, and economics. The ends must never be used to justify the means; the means and the ends must be in harmony. The process by which we accomplish our goal is an expression of our humanitarian and democratic values, and creating an effective, humane, and democratic process is itself the goal toward which we strive. Therefore, Ikeda's nonviolent humanism has as its goal the humanization of all institutions of power, the creation of the beloved world community.

Critics suggest that Ikeda should stick to talking about Buddhism and question why a spiritual leader would want to become involved with the United Nations or spend so much time establishing cultural institutions or universities. They suggest that he is doing so merely to gratify his own personal ambitions. Directly or indirectly, such criticisms attempt to force Ikeda to confine himself to realms of activity that others are more comfortable with and not to use his beliefs or values to call for meaningful engagement. But Ikeda sees the world differently, and so do I. If we recognize the reality of interdependence, then that unifying cosmic perspective has to inform the planetary human value system, especially if we are to deal with enormous issues such as global environmental protection.

I see myself walking with Jesus as a constructive iconoclast, trying to get to a new place with new means. That does not mean abandoning the old landmarks but rather seeing them in a new light. I espouse the ecumenism of Martin Luther King Jr. With the rise of the Christian Right and the proliferation of prosperity theology in both African American and white megachurches, however, I fear that the Christianity in America that I know and love is no longer a real force for peace. Indeed, a new light needs to shine from these sanctuaries—one that focuses on the possibility of achieving peace on this earth in our words and our deeds.

In the peace-building work of Daisaku Ikeda, I have found a light that shines as both a religious and secular beacon for peace. Thus, for the past nearly twenty years, I have joined hands with the SGI to form a most unlikely partnership, a Baptist minister and a Japanese lay Buddhist leader. I do this because I believe profoundly that coexistence requires interfaith leadership, and I want to stand in the vanguard. Also, at a time when the American Christian church has grown increasingly intolerant of religious diversity, equality, and liberty, the founding principles of our nation, I want to bring attention to the rich diversity and interfaith understanding and cooperation that I see illuminating the SGI.

I applaud any serious seeker of spirituality, and in my life as a Baptist I have also felt the freedom of conscience to learn from many different spiritual traditions. But perhaps there is something a little undisciplined when we style a set of beliefs from ideas we find appealing at the moment. Whether intentional or not, this could become a way to fashion a spirituality that does not challenge whatever worldview we already have and that therefore allows us to avoid grappling with new and challenging ideas. But that very grappling, that inner struggle, has always been at the heart of my own spiritual growth, and when I read the great spiritual teachers of my own Christian faith or other traditions, I see them, too, grappling with difficult ideas.

Spiritual growth is many things, but it is not easy. It does not come without effort, questions, doubts, sacrifice, revisions, redefinitions, and risk. The greatest spiritual teachers have grown not by avoiding commitment but by seeking it; not by rejecting a tradition or a community but by expanding perspectives and flourishing within them.

I am inspired by Daiskau Ikeda's ability to reach far beyond the confines of his small island nation and to spread his message the world over. He invites us to come from behind the fences that confine our hearts and minds. He shows us that to work for peace we must be prepared to get out of many boxes: academic, class, culture, diet, ethnic, gender, ideology, language, nationality, race, religion, and sexual orientation in order to pursue the truth.

Gandhi, King, and Ikeda had to think outside of their own faith, their race, their language, and their nationality in order to ground themselves in nonviolence. Gandhi, an Indian Hindu, dared to study and follow the ideas of the Russian novelist Leo Tolstoy. King, an African America in the southern United States, dared to study and follow the ideas of Gandhi. Ikeda, a Japanese Buddhist, has dared to embrace a multitude of diverse leaders and thinkers from around the globe, expressed in more than eighty published book-length dialogues.

I, too, had to be willing to get out of my African American and Baptist identity box in order to begin to understand the Soka Gakkai and its unique approach to peace activism. Had I decided early on that I, a black person practicing the religion of Jesus for some seven decades, simply could not relate to a religion rooted in the teachings of thirteenth-century Japan, I would have missed all of the spiritual enrichment the Soka Gakkai has brought to my life.

Upon entering the Atlanta SGI-USA Buddhist Center for the first time in 1999, I was greeted by stunning human diversity, uncommon for any American religious congregation. There were African Americans, Chinese, East Indians, Japanese, Peruvians, Puerto Ricans, South Africans, Southeast Asians, West Indians, and Euro-Americans. There, as if in a dream, I saw my mentor Martin Luther King Jr.'s vision of the beloved world house community come to life.

I am fascinated and positively impressed with the diversity—racial, ethnic, geographic, academic, and economic— of the SGI-USA membership. In SGI-USA, all are present: the sons and daughters of Christians of every denomination from Catholic to Unitarian, Jews, even Muslims who have found a new spiritual path in the practice of Nichiren Buddhism. Although I have preached and prayed in hundreds of churches and religious centers around the world, this was an energetic and beautiful unity I have witnessed in few other religious settings.

While Sunday morning at eleven o'clock remains the most segregated hour in America, SGI-USA has managed to transcend this country's legacy of race, class, and creed divisions to become the first strain of Eastern philosophy and religious practice to take serious hold by attracting a broad cross section of the population. *Tricycle* magazine, a popular Buddhist journal, credits the Soka Gakkai with being the most racially and ethnically diverse Buddhist community in the United States, an achievement no other

Buddhist sect or Eastern-based religion can claim. The SGI is building the world house that my mentor strove so mightily to construct.

By founding two universities and establishing a culture of dialogue, Daisaku Ikeda has made sure that he will have disciples long after he is gone. Not only is he ensuring that his own legacy of peace work continues, but more than anyone else alive, he is continuing the efforts of Gandhi and King. He is making the effort to ensure that the teachings of nonviolence are practiced by future generations. He is seeking to create institutions that will avoid the normalization of violence and that will keep the principles of peace and nonviolence alive in the hearts, minds, attitudes, behavior, policies, and institutions of future generations.

Many great men and women have aspired to meaningful social change, holding beautiful visions of an ideal community in their hearts. But as beautiful or significant as those visions are, they are lost over the generations because the original visionaries eventually pass on and no one is left to keep them alive. When those visionary ideals are left behind in written form to be read and studied, however, and when there are followers ready to keep them alive and institutions where they may be discussed and taught, they may continue to live in the world. This is the reason the Christian Scriptures were canonized after the Ascension of Jesus and the death of the firsthand witnesses of his transforming ministry—so that the stories would not be lost to unborn generations.

Gandhi and King were so busy leading and building their nonviolence movements and peace ministries for social change that they did not have time to build institutions to carry on the legacies of their work. I am sure that if their lives had not been tragically cut short, they would have turned their attention to the education of young people. It should be noted that Gandhi's ashrams and King's Southern Christian Leadership Conference offered models that both men wanted to expand upon in order to bring about greater social change.

Many of us are familiar with Gandhi's famous injunction to be the change we wish to see in the world. There are days when I seem to see this slogan everywhere—on bumper stickers, T-shirts, postcards, shopping bags, and on dorm room walls. Of course, I am delighted that such an important idea has become so commonplace in our society, and I hope that it means that there are more and more people who actually live their lives in this way. But this slogan is much more than a platitude; it is an expression of a way of life spoken by a man who knew exactly what he was saying, and exactly what he was asking of others.

If all we have left of men like Gandhi and King are statues and monuments, if the only remnants of their ideas are catchphrases or sayings that make us feel better, then their true legacies will be forgotten. Without a real knowledge of their histories and their struggles, and without fostering a commitment to embody the work they were engaged in, we truly have nothing left of these men at all.

When most Americans consider King, they probably think of him as one of the greatest leaders of the African American community, which he certainly was. Others regard him more broadly, as a great American who led one of the most important movements in our nation's history. I do not find fault with either of these characterizations of King. But for me, whether you view him as a great black leader or as a great American, both views are limited and do not do justice to the depth or range of his vision. For King, ending racism and inequality in the United States was an essential element of his vision, but it was not the sole aim of his work. Fighting injustice was a crucial step toward his larger goal of creating the beloved world community.

During one of King's most famous sermons, delivered on Christmas Eve, he said:

> If we are to have peace on Earth, our loyalties must become ecumenical rather than sectional. Our loyalties must transcend our race, our tribe, our class, and our nation; and this means we must develop a world perspective. No individual can live alone; no nation can live alone, and as long as we try, the more we are going to have war in this world.[43]

King's beloved community, his world house, was a vision of a completely integrated society, both locally and globally, a community of love and justice wherein brotherhood and sisterhood and ecological integrity would be an actuality in all of social life. This vision was rooted in his deep Christian faith.

Ikeda's view of global citizenship is rooted in his own Buddhist spirituality, but his ideal of global citizenship is, to my mind, the same as King's Christian ideals of love and humanity. Both men have pointed toward what Jason D. Hill refers to as "sociality," the championing of our global society's best interests.

Global citizens are people who possess the virtues of wisdom, courage, and compassion. As Ikeda writes, the essential elements of global citizenship are: "the wisdom to perceive the interconnectedness of all life and living; the courage not to fear or deny differences, but to respect and strive to understand people of different cultures and to grow from encounters with them; the compassion to maintain an imaginative empathy that reaches beyond one's immediate surroundings and extends to those suffering in distant places."[44] Global citizenship reveals itself in the capacity for cross-cultural cooperation and collaborative excellence. It is an expression of the Christian ideal of agape. Ikeda's ideal of global citizenship calls on young people to understand their responsibility to live ethically, to help others, even in distant places, and to leave something behind for the generations to come.

Human destiny is not fixed; fulfilling it does not mean to arrive at a set destination. Fulfilling our destiny means to live on the cutting edge of growth. All persons are in a perpetual state of becoming and revealing, always in the process of an evolutionary emergence. Education, in the sense of

Soka education, has a crucial role to play. Institutionalizing the process of evolutionary growth and being a "transformed nonconformist" is precisely the aim of the Soka schools, and of Soka University of Japan and America.

Ikeda has lived up to his mentor's call to build what could be called a beloved commonwealth of global citizens. I mean this phrase deliberately, and I intend for it to convey not only the community of the faithful who Ikeda certainly loves and has dedicated himself toward building but also to the beloved community that extends beyond any single faith community to inspire people who are moral cosmopolitans, whose ethics and spirituality are not narrow, partisan, or sectarian but that draw from the world and seek to enrich all of humanity.

Chapter Thirteen

An Inside Job

Nichiren Buddhism emphasizes self-transformation as the key to affecting harmony and peace in one's immediate surroundings—home, family, workplace, community, and, by extension, the world. In other words, peace is an inside job. This emphasis recalls the words of Jesus: "The kingdom of God is within you."[45] I am enriched by the SGI's ancient Buddhist philosophy linking personal inner transformation to peace on a global scale. It is this understanding that most connects what I learned from my first mentor away from home, Martin Luther King Jr., and what I am now learning from Daisaku Ikeda.

Martin Luther King's defining philosophy is known as personalism. This has been a movement in the fields of ethics, philosophy, and theology for more than a hundred years and expresses the idea of the inherent nobility of the individual person, and the responsibility of that person within community. Walter Muelder, Martin Luther King's tutor and my teacher at Boston University, stated that the "person" never really exists in pure isolation but is always "the person-in-community." Our personal rights and obligations always exist in a relational, social context. Our individual decisions always have social impact. Conversely, when we want to address social concerns, we must always look to our own personal choices.

In one of the first lectures I read by Ikeda, he talked about humanism, and I was immediately struck by how his ideas resonated with King's understanding. When Ikeda talks about Buddhist humanism, he is speaking of a conception of the individual human being—his or her inherent value, inherent rights, and inherent obligations—that requires a commitment to nonviolence. Ikeda's discussion of nonviolence, then, is rooted profoundly in his understanding of Buddhist humanism, which has much in common with King's conception of the person.

For both King and Ikeda the sacred dignity of each person is the point from which we have to start. For Ikeda, this is a truth that comes from his spiritual conviction that each person possesses the life state of Buddhahood. But such a view is also rooted in a Christian view. Thomas Merton, an American Roman Catholic Trappist monk, wrote: "If once we begin to recognize, humbly but truly, the real value of our own self, we would see that this value was the sign of God in our being, the signature of God upon our being."[46]

The spiritual writer and thinker Paul Elie explains, "In the lives of most of us, God's signature is shown to us in the love of others."[47] But whether we understand it as a Christian or a Buddhist, this idea is a crucial first principle in an extended philosophy of nonviolence.

Ikeda's Buddhist humanism focuses on the oppressed and the poor, using their conditions as an index of the health and justice of their society—and, by extension, of humanity as a whole. King's nonviolent personalism has a similar focus, fighting against the dehumanization and depersonalization of all people.

The SGI's practice of inner self-reformation answers the question that students who arrive in the Gandhi-King-Ikeda course I teach at Morehouse inevitably find themselves asking, "What does it take to be able to practice nonviolence in a world that grows more violent every day?"

"If you focus outside of yourself," I reply, "you are just moving furniture around on the deck of the *Titanic*. The ship will go down anyway because the problem is inside of you. Peace is an inside job. Divinity, the sacredness of life, is within you. This reaching to practice nonviolence is an evolution. But you cannot evolve unless you are evolving from something, from the acorn within the oak. If you are coming from a conscious awareness of your own divinity, that is what you are going to give off. That is what everyone will feel and see. You have to affirm life beginning with your own. And so, if you feel you have problems or issues that have not been baptized in acceptance, it does not matter what exterior grooming you do. Nothing about your behavior will change. You must discover that every so-called problem comes with a gift hidden within it. Consider the rich maroon cherries—juicy, ripe, sweet. But they come with hard pits inside of them. The pits symbolize our hidden belief in limitations; if revealed those pits will transmute into love, faith, optimism, thinking, wisdom, compassion, action, forgiveness, and new possibilities."

This answer, however, is often hard for my students to grasp. Why? Because young people tend to be more tuned into the outside world, not the interior world of their own lives, the state of their own hearts and minds. Still, I believe they are seeking the teaching and the tools that can guide them in the process of inner spiritual reformation that begins within. From there, it can ripple out to their immediate environments and beyond, ultimately creating the macro-transformation that actually leads to real peace in the world.

One of the first chapel assistants arrived at Morehouse a biblical fundamentalist, strongly homophobic and misogynistic. Early on, he was helping me with communion as one of the chapel assistants, another of whom that day was a female chapel assistant from a neighboring college. I blessed the bread and I blessed the wine. I put the bread on a plate and passed them to the chapel assistants to distribute. But when I prepared to hand the bread plate to the young woman, my male student reached around the female chapel assistant and took it from me. Later, when I questioned him why he had done this, he replied that my female chapel assistant would have contaminated the plate if she had touched it, because of her gender.

This young man carried around a big Bible and he talked with that Bible, wagging it in your face. He shook it at me as we spoke together. With that Bible he condemned women, and he condemned homosexuality. Of course, I had my own thoughts about him even then. Methinks he did protest too much. One of the most serious kinds of violence is the intimate violence that occurs when we disrespect other people's humanity because we find it difficult to honor our own—because it is hard to accept who we are. I have a long track record of accepting homosexuals at Morehouse, but this young man could not open up to me. He could not open up to himself.

Still, he reached out to me from time to time. I received a call from him one day when he was at graduate school. He was having some trouble, although it wasn't clear to me exactly what it was. He was a dorm director and something had happened with some of the residents in his dorm. I began to think it was probably sexual, but I was not sure. He dropped out and I later found out that he had tried to commit suicide by running his car off the road. It was a bad accident, but he lived, after which he had to come to terms with the mess his life had become.

One hot summer day, he came to see me. He was back in graduate school, working on a terminal degree at a major research university. That's when he told me about his suicide attempt and the counseling that helped him come to terms with the fact that he was gay and had been running away from who he was. For a long time he simply could not accept it. He was a Pentecostal from Mississippi. The whole environment he had grown up in told him that homosexuality was wrong, a sin.

Once he had experienced his *own* human revolution and come to terms with who he was, he was ready to affect real change in the world and to become a messenger for peace.

In the Soka Gakkai, the term *human revolution* was first used by Ikeda's lifelong mentor, Josei Toda. I have no doubt that in the twenty-first century the term *human revolution* will take root in the American spiritual vernacular. Human revolution, as I have come to understand it, means an inner reformation from ignorance of one's own inner divinity to a profound awareness of the Buddha or Christ nature within—from selfishness to selflessness, from limited prospects to limitless possibilities.

This rapid change in one's fundamental being occurs by overcoming personal adversities, internal and external. Ikeda calls it breaking "the hard shell of the lesser self" to reveal "a greater self," a self more capable of wisdom and compassionate action. We Christians might think of human revolution as being "born again" . . . Nichiren Buddhist style. Or we might think of Jesus. His forty days and forty nights in the wilderness propelled his own human revolution; when he emerged, he was a changed person.

As SGI practitioners accumulate a personal record with their own human revolution—changing on the inside in order to change their outer environment—they develop faith in their ability to transform even the most daunting, negative circumstances into positive value and creative benefit for themselves and others. This experience "dispels any feeling of powerlessness. It teaches a dynamic way of living in which we breathe the immense life of the universe itself," says Ikeda. "It teaches the true great adventure of self-reformation."[48] By extension, by focusing both inwardly and outwardly on peace, SGI practitioners grow increasingly more confident that humankind has the potential to overcome conflicts by applying the theory and practice of human revolution.

At the core of the human revolution process is the Nichiren Buddhist belief in the Mystic Law: the unchanging truth of the sacredness of all human life, the idea that we each have "some sky in us," that we all have God inside. Because of that truth, we as ordinary human beings are capable of the discipline and spiritual genius it takes to make peace real on the planet. The Mystic Law holds within it the vibratory truth that humankind can be in up-leveled consciousness and in sync with the universe and can in fact—by our very thoughts, words, deeds, and chants—change our destiny from one of violence to one of peace. Thus, Ikeda and his value-creation practitioners do not abdicate responsibility for the future of humanity to an outside force. It is simply up to us.

As a Christian, I want to join Ikeda and the Buddhists in not leaving the responsibility for peace up to God alone. The SGI has helped deepen my understanding that Jesus is more of a practitioner than a preacher. Of course, Christ was a teacher. But Christians believe in God and literally worship Jesus. Buddhists think that is the wrong approach; they believe in the Mystic Law of the sacredness of all human beings. What Christians do not realize is that Jesus did not want to be worshipped. He wanted to be emulated. He wanted to be followed. He wanted his teachings to be obeyed—meaning, he wanted them to take root deep in the lives of people. He wanted a new kingdom to come from within.

I am reminded of Jesus's saying "Greater works than these will he do."[49] This is a tremendous expression of humility on the part of Jesus. For me, it confirms my acceptance of Jesus as my example. As I see it, Jesus does not save us. Rather, he frees us so that we can save ourselves. Through our thoughts, words, deeds, and prayers, we can do even greater works than he. Taking Jesus at his word is a freeing proposition.

Martin Luther King Jr. traveled far to learn about love, and he traveled far to put it into action. King did not just hear the call to love; he strove throughout his days to put it into practice, even in the midst of his most difficult social battles. When King walked into a room, he conferred love on all the people in the room. He knew the sacredness of all human life and decided to come from a place of love. His strategy was to live from the inside out, embodying the values he preached. When he did not see those values in the world around him, this only emboldened his determination to embody them and bestow them upon the world.

We have to be free of negativity in order to give love. But we must have self-love in order to do this. King made an intention to give love no matter what negativity or violence he met. He respected everyone's humanity, even affirming the personhood of his oppressors.

In a famous sermon delivered at the Dexter Avenue Baptist Church in Montgomery, Alabama, in 1957, King asked, "How do you go about loving your enemies?" The answer he gave was: "In order to love your enemies, you must begin by analyzing self. And I am sure that seems strange to you, that I start out telling you this morning that you love your enemies by beginning with a look at self."[50]

For King, as with Ikeda, the act of self-reflection is not some narcissistic act. It is an honest appraisal of ourselves and our motives and how our behavior has affected others. King said:

> We must face the fact that an individual might dis-like us because of . . . some personality attribute that we possess, something that we've done deep down in the past and we have forgotten about it; but it was that something that aroused the hate response within the individual. That is why I say, begin with yourself. There might be something within you that arouses the tragic hate response in the other individual.[51]

The honest effort to reflect on ourselves is an act that requires the virtue of courage. More than this, it allows us to move beyond feeling victimized by what others have done to us and gives us the power to realize that our own behavior has an effect on other people for good or for bad.

Loving our enemies requires us to respond to a higher moral calling. It requires us to reflect on ourselves and change our behavior. It is an act of self-mastery. In this sense, love, in the Kingian sense, requires action and courage. It was Carl G. Jung who said, "The world hangs on a thin thread; and that thread is the human psyche." Our capacity to subdue hatred and to overcome violence in the world is first and foremost the effort to do this within our own lives.

When Ikeda and King talk about peace, they are talking about a world free of violence that is an expression of the effort within each of us to overcome our own impediments. What is the basis for genuine peace? It is total freedom, total inner freedom.

We humans cannot experience peace unless we are free: free of addiction; free of anger or grudge; free of anxiety, hopelessness, fear, or depression; free of victimhood; free from being unforgiving; free from wanting to exact revenge; free from self-deception; free from denial, projection, and avoidance. Freedom means being free from self-imposed negative beliefs, from old stories that limit and confine us. When we are free of these things, all of life has the opportunity to manifest as love.

The totality of Ikeda's commitment to this process and his firm belief in its capacity to effect peace in real and concrete terms is contained in the following quote in the preface to his novel, *The Human Revolution*, "A great human revolution in just a single individual will help achieve a change in the destiny of a nation and, further, will enable a change in the destiny of all humankind."[52]

In other works, when Ikeda discusses what this "great human revolution" entails, he says that "our task is to establish a firm inner world, a robust sense of self that will not be swayed or shaken by the most trying of circumstances or pressing adversity. Only when efforts to reform society have as their point of departure the reformation of the inner life—human revolution—will they lead us with certainty to a world of lasting peace and true human security."[53]

What Ikeda refers to as self-reformation is another way of referring to our human aspiration to seek to live truest to what is best within us. But this effort to realize our fullest potential necessarily includes a call to help one another— our friends and neighbors, and even our so-called enemies, whom we are called to love just as we would love ourselves. Martin Luther King Jr. said, "I can never be what I ought to be until you are what you ought to be; and you can never be what you ought to be until I am what I ought to be."[54]

In Ikeda and the SGI I see the ultimate spiritual pragmatists, equipping people in all walks of life with the spiritual texts, tools, and community to do the work that brings about personal realization of enlightenment, collective action, and advocacy for peace. In so doing, they demonstrate a spiritual genius that I have not seen anywhere else. Through my association with them, I have been delivered from the days when I despaired over my inability to perpetuate the legacy of my mentor Martin Luther King Jr.'s philosophy of nonviolence.

One of the most significant things the SGI has done for the King Chapel is move with speed, urging me to overcome my feelings of powerlessness and regret to believe that now is the time to spread the good news of nonviolence, happiness, care, harmony, cooperation, justice, sustainability, and peace. The SGI's presence at the chapel is like the eagle who flew over the chicken yard: I felt the wind from its mighty wings. They lifted me from inertia and frustration and propelled me into vibrant action. Daisaku Ikeda and the Soka Gakkai International gave my faith wings of renewed hope that peace, even in the midst of these increasingly terrifying, violent, and war-mongering times, is a drumbeat worth marching to.

I embraced Martin Luther King Jr. as my mentor more than half a century ago, and Mohandas K. Gandhi three decades ago. But upon learning of the life and work of Daisaku Ikeda, I felt compelled to declare that I had found a third world-class, spiritual master. And this is why I, a black Baptist minister whose soul is hewn out of the mountain of racial injustice that is the birthright of every African American, have chosen to become a disciple of a Japanese Buddhist who speaks no English, and hold him in high esteem, just as I hold Martin Luther King Jr., one of the greatest men to have walked the earth.

Chapter Fourteen

Faith to Heal the World

I was born on a Tuesday, September 23, 1941, at 5:25 p.m. I had been in the world only five days, and on that fifth day, my family took me to the Shiloh Missionary Baptist Church in Dawson, Georgia, Terrell County. This county was sometimes called terrible Terrell. It had a history of being the cruelest county to African Americans in the nation. At the end of the Sunday morning sermon, my grandmother, without saying anything to anyone about what she was about to do, took me in her arms, walked down the aisle, stood before the congregation, and prayed aloud, "Lord, make this boy a preacher."

That was the first prayer ever prayed over me. "Lord, make this boy a preacher."

It had a startling effect on the congregation. Yet no one said a word to me about it until January 1977, when I was a grown man, in my thirties, and finally an ordained preacher, married, and graduated from Boston University School of Theology. I was sitting with my family in my mother's living room in Columbus, Ohio, and we were discussing our family history as we watched the historic

ABC television premier of Alex Haley's *Roots*, the saga of an African American family's journey from Africa through the Middle Passage to slavery and to freedom. During one of the commercials, my mother turned to me to tell me the story. "When you were born," she said, "your grandmother prayed for you aloud in front of the entire congregation, 'Lord, make this boy a preacher.'" The news stunned me so completely that I had to leave the house for a walk alone.

I did not know about my grandmother's prayer, but I had learned to love going to church with her when I was a little boy living in her home. I did not know about my grandmother's prayer, but as a teenager I yearned to understand the Bible. I did not know about my grandmother's prayer, but from the ninth grade the idea started growing stronger and stronger in me that I should prepare for college to be a pastor of a church.

My grandmother, my aunt, my mother, and my pastor made no suggestions, exerted no influence. But they watched and supported me as my childhood interests grew and developed. They trusted in the power of prayer. My achievements are not accidents. I believe that the hopes and prayers of so many people have been behind every accomplishment in my life. Hamlet was right when he said: "There's a divinity that shapes our ends / Rough-hew them how we will."[55]

My grandmother died in 1946 of a cerebral hemorrhage when I was five years old. As she lay on her deathbed in our Terrell County house on South Walnut Street, the last words she spoke to me were "Be a good boy," as I was being held over her bed in the arms of my maternal uncle, Nena Mullins, whom I called Uncle Mud. This was my first encounter with a family member's death. Uncle Mud had prepared me when he came to take me into the bedroom of Madear. He said, "Your grandmother is going to be leaving us, so I am taking you to her." I recall my anxiety as I feared that I would not get to see Madear after that night. My little mind did not want to believe that death was something that could happen to my madear. She was the first mother that I had consistently known, because my biological mother, Bernice, was a part of the Great Migration, north and west, to secure employment in the 1940s. My madear's final words have had great power in my life. Somehow, mysteriously, even before I knew it, I always wanted to become the person my grandmother hoped and prayed that I would be. I still constantly think about her funeral and burial.

My grandmother was a widow who earned a pittance cooking and ironing in the houses of white families where she was not even allowed to use the same toilet as her employer. But she served for many years as the president of the church's missionary society, and she knew the power of prayer. When I visit her grave, I take a hoe and a rake and clear the weeds from around the tombstone for Willie Mae Roberts Childs Mullins. And I hold a little graveside service for her in gratitude for prophesying my destiny.

My path as a Baptist preacher and dean of the chapel was preordained by Willie Mae Mullins, the matriarch of my family and a woman of stalwart vision. This, among many other revelations over the course of my lifetime, is why I know my soul belongs to Jesus. And it is precisely because of my profound conviction in the teachings of Jesus the Christ, the Prince of Peace, that I want to raise up the Nichiren Buddhist peace movement of the twelve-million strong Soka Gakkai International movement and its leader Daisaku Ikeda. As an ordained minister, I know the power of prayer. It is not empty, and it is not weak; quite the contrary. When prayer expresses a deep hope or aspiration, when it expresses a profound longing from within, it calls us toward a more transcendent and courageous way of living. It is the most powerful evidence of God in my life.

The SGI promotes a consistent daily practice—a recitation of the mantra Nam-myoho-renge-kyo to a mandala called the Gohonzon. I see this practice as a powerful combination of meditation and prayer. I have always understood prayer to be a form of luxuriating in the qualities of God, of supplication, of humbling oneself before God, and in that Infinite Presence, to express myself most meaningfully to the Infinite. In this sense, prayer is a kind of collaboration as well as an experience of communion, of seeking to join with (to be in vibrational alinement with) what is most holy, harmonious, perfect, and true. But I understand that in Buddhism, the daily devotions are regarded as a way to summon the ultimate from deep within, a rousing of strength and spirit, a personal call to action.

Superficially, the Christian view of prayer appears to be outwardly directed, while Buddhist prayer seems to be inwardly focused. I suppose that those apparent differences might spark an interesting theoretical discussion on the differences between Christian and Buddhist ways to pray. But I think that in reality, in actual practice, prayer always has elements of both.

SGI members seek communion with the universal Dharma, or Mystic Law, through reciting their mantra in front of their Gohonzon, the calligraphic scroll that is the "object of devotion" for all Nichiren Buddhists. And we Christians do not pray passively, asking for some superheroic force or "cosmic bellhop" outside of us to solve all our problems for us while we sit back and do nothing. When we pray or chant sincerely and intentionally knowing that what we are seeking has already been given, and that we as Buddhists and Christians alike are engaged in the art of vibrational increase and alignment with the name, nature, and qualities of ultimacy, then our perspective ought to be changed. And when this happens, our actions also change. When we pray confidently, we experience utopia.

For Christians, God is not a problem solver. There are no problems in God. In God all problems dissolve, because the omniactive, omniabundant, omnipresent spirit corresponds and responds to its own nature reflected and vibrating in our prayers and chanting. When we pray for peace in our communities, we are called upon to reflect upon the Infinite, and in the process, to reflect upon ourselves. And from this reflection, we are called upon to live in ways that embody our deepest aspirations for peace.

As a Christian and a scholar of religion, I have learned from Daisaku Ikeda's personal understanding of prayer. His devotion to his faith has been a source of encouragement and inspiration to me in my personal faith, and I am grateful to him for this.

Ikeda's perspective on the purpose of prayer is best expressed in something he wrote about the Buddha, the founder of Buddhism, known in Asia as Shakyamuni but more commonly in the West as Gautama Siddhartha. Ikeda wrote:

> Shakyamuni was a man who lived some twenty-five hundred years ago in central northern India and who earnestly and untiringly sought to discover the nature of the dharma, or Law, the eternal principles of truth that transcend time and place. He was a thinker of giant proportions who, for the sake of people in ages to come, persisted in his efforts to discover the source of creation and to free human existence from all impediments.[56]

The meditative practice Shakyamuni explored, and the truth of life to which he became enlightened, was the "eternal" that transcended time and place, and was "the source of all creation." The purpose of the Buddha's effort was to free himself, and by extension, all humanity "from all impediments."

It seems to me that these "impediments" are whatever block us from "the source of all creation," that keep us from knowing the "eternal principles." They are to Buddhists internal sources of negativity—self-doubt, desire, attachment, or fear. These correspond to what many Christians would call the Devil, Satan, Lucifer, Beelzebub, or simply the Tempter. They express our human capacity to do harm to one another, to behave from a place of hatred or naked self-interest. They are what is evil in human nature, what we Christians call sin or moral evil.

When Ikeda refers to impediments, he refers to those qualities internal to each of us, intrinsic to human nature, which keep us mean, which root us in shallow and selfish desires to be satisfied by any means, and which—as a society—cause us to value self-interest over the common good. In a Christian context, these impediments stand in the way of our living Christ's call to love one another; they cause us to feel separate from one another, and therefore they separate us from God. From my Christian perspective, I believe Jesus lived to free us so we could save ourselves.

"[War] is the source of all evil," Ikeda writes. "War normalizes insanity—the kind that does not hesitate to destroy human beings like so many insects, and tears all that is human and humane to shreds, producing an unending stream of refugees. It also cruelly damages our natural environment."[57] And elsewhere, "Nothing is more tragic and cruel than war."[58]

In this way of understanding, war is simply the most

pronounced manifestation of those "impediments" or that "evil" that lies within each of us. Overcoming this evil within, subduing the Satanic inherent in our lives, is, in this sense, the purpose of prayer and the only way to establish peace.

For Ikeda, like Ralph Waldo Emerson, opening the path to peace is fundamentally not a matter of intellect but a matter of character, of the exercise of self-restraint and the willingness to act or live our virtue. "Character is higher than intellect,"[59] as Emerson said. The intellect can grow and grow, with the limits of knowledge, in persons who remain crude, cruel, rude, smug, and even ungenerous. Such intellects produced the Holocaust, American slavery, apartheid, the atomic bombing of Japan, the "shock and awe" war on Iraq, water poisoning in Flint, Michigan, and the Soviet Gulag. Martin Heidegger, a brilliant philosopher, Paul De Man, a prominent literary critic and poet, and Ezra W. L. Pound, an immortal poet and critic, all tied themselves to the hate of Fascism and Nazism that marked the 1930s. Professors, doctors, lawyers, judges, journalists, schoolteachers, and clergy accommodated themselves to the political power of murderous thugs. All of this intellectual professional knowledge and tacit sanctioning of moral evil raises one question: "What is the point of *knowing* good if you do not keep trying to *become* a good person?" There are clear limits to abstract knowledge. Moral reasoning is not the same as moral behavior. We attend school to grow from moral analysis and study to realized moral commitment and living. But we all know that the study of philosophy—moral philosophy or moral reasoning—cosmopolitan ethics, cosmopolitan theology, or the theology of world religions will not prompt the teacher or the student to embody a determination to live in accordance with ethical principles or options.

Maybe the best way to connect intellect to character is through community service. This can make real our understandings of abstract disciplines, affect attitudes toward so-called ghetto clinics, churches, schools, civil society agencies, and their citizens whose lives also matter, and strengthen our sense of caring.

Prayer plays an essential role in allowing us to develop what the Buddhists might refer to as "self-mastery," the inner qualities necessary to subdue what is darkest within each of us and to demonstrate the courage to live true to the values we espouse. This is an important perspective on prayer for anyone, of any faith tradition. We must learn to live in the results for which we pray. We must live according to what is possible in the outcome. If our prayers for peace are genuine, then we must learn to live the action of peace, and to make the effort for peace, knowing that peace itself is the way. The US Defense Department should be renamed the US Peace Department.

I know many Christians who, like myself, pray daily. But I know many others who pray only occasionally, in passing, or only on those occasions when they go to church services. As a Christian minister, however, I am truly impressed by the earnest effort in prayer I see being made by the members of the SGI. It is only matched in its frequency by the Muslims. I am acquainted with Buddhists, and I know that a consistent and robust daily practice is one of the key elements of their spiritual life. The daily devotional practice carried out by SGI members is a reflection of their commitment to the growth of their own integrity of character and their ever-expanding sense of what they are capable of achieving. But when I observe them in their practice, I also perceive them as engaged in a fierce battle to defeat their inner darkness and negativity. On this level, too, I find myself inspired and renewed in my efforts to pray—not out of formality but out of my spontaneous and consistently renewed commitment to become a better person.

Nonviolent resistance is not a passive nonresistance to evil (which is really an acceptance of evil) but is the active nonviolent resistance to evil. If people use nonviolent resistance because they are afraid, or because they lack the instruments of violence, such people are cowardly or calculating but are not truly nonviolent. Nonviolent resistance refuses to accept the conditions of injustice it seeks to change. Gandhi's movement to overthrow British colonial rule in India demonstrated that nonviolent resistance is not a method for cowards. It does not fight, but that does not make it weak or rooted in fear.

Gandhi demonstrated that nonviolent resistance is an attack directed against the forces of evil rather than against the persons who are doing the evil. It is the purpose of nonviolence to defeat evil ideas or dehumanizing or oppressive functions, not to demonize or vilify people. It does not seek to humiliate the opponent but attempts to win their friendship and understanding, thereby creating a community of agreement between resister and opponent.

Violence—even violent speech—creates an atmosphere of tragic bitterness between the two parties. Though the nonviolent resister must often express protest through noncooperation or boycotts, these are not ends in themselves. They are merely a way to awaken a sense of moral regret and self-reflection in the opponent. The end is redemption and reconciliation. The aftermath of violence is always tragic bitterness, but the aftermath of nonviolent resistance is the creation of the beloved world community. "Nonviolence is a weapon fabricated of love. It is a sword that heals,"[60] wrote King.

Because nonviolent resistance avoids both external physical and internal emotional, intimate, spiritual violence, it is an expression of the ideal of love as agape. It is that love which makes no distinction between friend and so-called enemy, which loves all people simply because of their need to be loved, the love that is dynamic and willing to go the extra mile, forgiving and loving everyone, and that believes that all women and men are sisters and brothers. For the Christians, Jesus, whom we through faith call the Christ, is the ground, goal, norm, and motive for responsible community and its realization. The perfection and unconditional love of Christ motivates. Hence, the cosmopolitan community of loving concern is a community without barriers. The love of God as demonstrated in Jesus is not simply a memory or goal; it is a present relationship, which inspires, motivates, and sustains.

Resisting in this way—by refusing to acquiesce but also by refusing to pick up the tools of violence to strike out or tear down—requires self-discipline and an embodied humanitarian solidarity, what the South Africans call *ubuntu*. It requires strength and endurance and a sensitivity to or knowledge of ethical pluralism, that is, "the idea that there are many theories about what is 'right' and 'wrong' (moral norms) which may be incompatible and/or incommensurable with your own personal moral norms."[61] And it requires moral courage. Nonviolent resistance is the willingness to accept suffering without retaliation. The resister is willing to accept violence if necessary, but never to inflict it. Suffering has a powerful educational and transformative influence on men and women, on both the perpetrator and victim.

"We will win our freedom because the sacred heritage of our nation and the eternal will of God are embodied in our echoing demands,"[62] wrote Martin Luther King Jr. Nonviolent resistance is a spiritual and religious experience because its realization binds practitioners to the source. To believe that nonviolent resistance can work, you have to be convinced that God, or the universe, the Mystic Law, ultimately work to bring disconnected aspects of reality into a harmonious vibratory whole.

These Gandhian ideas influenced King profoundly, and we see in them a commitment to recognizing what is most divine and noble in others, and to act based on our own divinity and inner nobility, as Jesus did.

Ikeda has said, "We are charged with the task of not merely achieving a 'passive peace'—the absence of war—but of transforming on a fundamental level those social structures that threaten human dignity. Only in this way can we realize the positive, active values of peace. Efforts to enhance international cooperation and the fabric of international law are, of course, necessary. Even more vital are the creative efforts of individuals to develop a multilayered and richly patterned culture of peace, for it is on this foundation that a new global society can be built."[63]

But even with his emphasis on building strong institutions, cultivating a respect for the interdependence of all life, and recognizing the importance of courageous and controversial dialogue as a method for promoting peace, the focus for Ikeda is always the individual human being. And it is not just governments or political entities that must be focused on the well-being of each individual. All institutions of human endeavor must have this aim. This is especially true of religious institutions, because individual spiritual growth is an essential prerequisite for the establishment of lasting peace necessary to achieve the beloved world community.

The Buddhist form of prayer—the inwardly directed practice aimed at self-mastery—has something to teach us about the power of love. The Christian call to love, the effort to strive to help others become true to their ideal of personality, their ideal of world community, and their ideal norm requires of us to commit to self-reflection and personal growth. Love is a wonderful ideal norm, but to live up to that ideal requires effort and requires us to cross-examine and improve ourselves. We must find within ourselves a faith mighty enough to change the world.

Not too long ago I was hosting a conference of a thousand SGI members at the King Chapel. Unfortunately, there was a storm and the transformer at the chapel blew, so we had to move the entire event to the Forbes Basketball Arena at Morehouse, a facility that was built for the Olympics. Our chapel seats twenty-five hundred, but the arena is made for more than fifty-five hundred. With so much extra space, we all clustered to one side of the gymnasium for our program.

We were listening to the first speaker when a Morehouse policeman beckoned me to leave, whispering that he needed to speak to me.

"I hate to tell you this," he said, almost apologetically. "But we've just received a report from the weather bureau that a tornado is headed to Atlanta. Morehouse is in its direct path."

My first thought was how strange. Tornadoes seldom threaten the hearts of major cities. I looked up at the crowd. "How far away is it?" I asked.

"Very close," he answered.

"What should we do?"

"First, you must move this entire crowd away from that wall." He pointed to the side of the gym where more than a thousand souls had gathered for the meeting. (We have a large color picture of this gathering on the wall of the King Chapel library. So we will not forget this scene.)

I walked up to the speaker and asked for the microphone. "Stop the program," I said. "May I have your attention, please. I have an emergency announcement. I need your full cooperation."

I repeated what the policeman had relayed to me and everyone became utterly quiet and motionless. "I need everybody seated near that wall to move toward the center of the gym as quickly as you can. Please do that now."

To my complete amazement nobody moved. The whole audience sat frozen, staring at me. I waited, and watched, and I waited. The lights hanging from chains from the high ceiling were beginning to sway. Outside the wind was starting to howl and actually shake the west wall of the massive building.

I turned to an SGI leader seated in front of me and asked, somewhat helplessly, "Why are they ignoring me?"

"Because they are chanting," he answered.

"They're chanting the storm away?"

"Yes!" he said with great conviction. "They are chanting the storm around Morehouse College." This was the first time in my life I witnessed SGI members chanting silently.

The arena was completely still. You could not hear a word. The chanting was completely inaudible. A thousand-plus people, all focused, were praying as intently as they could. They had been trained in what to do. They knew what to do. Immediately after my announcement they went directly into their well-practiced spiritual prayer consciousness.

The lights were swinging wildly back and forth by now, rattling on their chains. The wall was beginning to shake more now. I feared that the large windows would break. People turned their heads. They could see it. "Move! NOW!" I said firmly in a commanding authoritarian Baptist preacher voice into the microphone. And they stood slowly, and then moved gracefully. Very slowly. People who were sitting further in did not move at all. It was very orderly, very calm. Yet it was a historic spiritual moment in my ecumenical interfaith journey as the founding dean of the Martin Luther King Jr. International Chapel. It was the first time I had ever seen a spiritual tool of a faith community collectively applied to a weather event. The National Weather Service reported that over the twenty-four-hour period of March 14–15, 2008, forty-five tornadoes were confirmed from eastern Alabama to the Carolina coast with most of the activity concentrated in the metropolitan Atlanta area, the Central Savannah River Area, and the Midlands of South Carolina. They reported that the tornado with winds of 135 mph, which cut a six-mile path of death and destruction, went around Morehouse and the Atlanta University Center Consortium and ripped into the heart of downtown Atlanta, causing major window damage to one of the tallest hotels in the world, the Westin Peachtree Plaza, and glass flew everywhere, raining down on the streets of downtown

Atlanta. But not one person was killed from the flying glass. Three people were killed and fifty-three people were injured but not in Atlanta, with $250 million of damage.

When the centurion came to Jesus and said, "I am not worthy that thou shouldest come under my roof: but speak the word only, and my servant shall be healed," Jesus said, "I have not found so great faith, no, not in Israel."[64]

That is the faith that more than one thousand SGI members demonstrated that day. The atmospheric pressure shifted; the tornado changed direction and went around Morehouse College. Everyone in the city was safe, and I knew it was because of the power of chanting. I knew it was because of the power of prayer.

There are storms of violence on the horizon, but we will look to the future with courage and imagination like my grandmother did. We will face the tornadoes and together we will pray and chant for peace.

Nichiren had his disciples in his day, and in the twentieth century, Nichiren's work was taken up by Tsunesaburo Makiguchi. Makiguchi had a disciple to carry on his legacy in Josei Toda. And Toda had Daisaku Ikeda. Now, Ikeda has his disciples, and I consider myself among them. I know that's quite a leap. Hopefully a quantum leap toward cosmic peace.

Ikeda is a Buddhist and the leader of an international Buddhist organization, and I am a Baptist preacher committed to Jesus and to my ministry of unconditional love and all-conditional responsibility. Ikeda is the founder of many cultural and educational institutions, while what I have founded is at Morehouse College. Ikeda is ninety and I am in my seventies. But I still say: as Gandhi had his King, and King has his Ikeda, Ikeda shall have his Carter.

I do not intend to fill Ikeda's shoes but rather to follow his example, and within the limits of my ability and the scope of the opportunities I have been given, I hope to do my part to carry on the message of the new superpowers, peace and nonviolence, to share the good word that we are all brothers and sisters sharing one world house, one global village that, working together, we can make beautiful by putting humanity first. My intention is to assist in the construction of the rainbow bridge of interfaith understanding and moral cosmopolitan cooperation. By so doing, God willing, I will help Ikeda in bringing about, at last, global peace on earth, and hopefully one day a world in which the person is valued supremely beyond the boundaries of nation states.

Afterword

The Gandhi, King, Ikeda Exhibition

Mohandas K. Gandhi, Martin Luther King Jr., and Daisaku Ikeda, three men from three different cultures and continents, followed a common path of profound dedication and achievement in improving the lives of all people.

In 1999 and 2000, I began to formulate the idea of creating an exhibition that would introduce the nonviolent movements of Gandhi, King, and Ikeda to a broader audience. I wanted it to be an exhibition that could travel the world and speak to a global audience. This was a natural extension of the work I had been doing for years at the Martin Luther King Jr. International Chapel.

The Legacy of Peace Project was a natural outgrowth of my efforts to keep King's writing and his nonviolence movement meaningful and visible in our multicultural and diverse global age. Coretta Scott King made this request of me the summer of 1979 when I arrived in Atlanta from Boston, where I had earlier in the decade helped her host trustees of the Martin Luther King Jr. Center for Nonviolent Social Change for their annual meeting. I have been involved with this exhibition for some eighteen years and have traveled the world to share my perspective on the teaching and practice of nonviolence, and the legacies that these three exemplars share.

"Gandhi, King, Ikeda: A Legacy of Building Peace" conveyed the themes and pivotal principles in the lives of these giants of the twentieth century. The exhibition panels featured colorful photographs, inspiring quotes, and factual information about Mahatma Gandhi, Martin Luther King Jr., and Daisaku Ikeda. While walking around the free-standing, S-curved walls, viewers could take in the wondrous lives of these three individuals.

The exhibition has five sections that each describes a theme common to the experiences of the three. The first section, Forging Destiny, describes how each man had a mentor. Gandhi had Henry David Thoreau for political strategy; his parents and the Hindu Baghavad Gita for spirituality; and Leo Tolstoy to show him the infinite power of love.

Martin Luther King had his father Martin Luther King Sr.; Morehouse College president Benjamin E. Mays; Howard Thurman, who was dean of chapel at Howard and Boston Universities; and Mordecai Wyatt Johnson, who introduced him to Gandhi.

Ikeda had his immediate mentor, Josei Toda, and Thoreau who showed him the importance of commitment to one's beliefs.

The section Humanity at the Heart depicts how Gandhi, King, and Ikeda's core beliefs in humanity's innate dignity and unlimited potential motivated them to work whole-heartedly for the sake of people.

The Principles Into Action section explains how each individual was able to create a positive, lasting influence on humanity by translating their lofty ideals into concrete actions.

Then the section Adversity and Resistance depicts how each turned challenging situations into catalysts for advancement based on the fifth and very important section, Nonviolence, which discusses how each individual shunned the use of violence and relied on peaceful methods to create social change.

As I traveled the world with the exhibition (see the Appendix B for details), my work was supported by the local SGI organizations in each city, and many of their young men and women volunteered their time to help make it a success. What impressed me most was their genuine commitment to interpersonal nonviolent social change, and without exception the young men and women I met told me their commitment was inspired by their mentor, Daisaku Ikeda. "Mine too," I often said.

My ultimate hope was that by examining the lives of these great figures, viewers of that exhibition and readers of this book, will find these lofty ideals and principles within their grasp in the midst of their own daily existence. For it is within the mundane realm of daily living that Mohandas K. Gandhi, Martin Luther King Jr., and Daisaku Ikeda have sought to forge an existence filled with dignity, freedom, and happiness for all people.

Appendix A

Gandhi, King, Ikeda Community Builders Prize Recipients

2001 HRH Prince El Hassan bin Talal
Prince of Jordan
President, The Club of Rome
Venue: Morehouse College—Atlanta, Georgia
Date: April 8, 2001

2001 Mr. Nelson R. Mandela
Former President, Republic of South Africa
Former President, African National Congress
Corecipient, Nobel Peace Prize, 1993
Venue: Nelson Mandela Foundation—Johannesburg, South Africa
Date: August 4, 2004

2001 Mr. Mikhail S. Gorbachev
Former President, the Soviet Union
President, The Gorbachev Foundation
President, Green Cross International
Recipient, Nobel Peace Prize, 1990
(Fell ill en route to the United States)

2002 Dr. Michael Nobel
Chairman, Nobel Family Society
Chairman, The Nonviolence Project
Venue: Morehouse College—Atlanta, Georgia
Date: April 7, 2002

2003 Ms. Betty Williams
Peace worker
Founder and President, World Centers of Compassion
  for Children
Corecipient, Nobel Peace Prize, 1977
Venue: Morehouse College—Atlanta, Georgia
Date: April 4, 2003

2004 Mr. F.W. De Klerk
Former President, Republic of South Africa
Corecipient, Nobel Peace Prize, 1993
Venue: Morehouse College—Atlanta, Georgia
Date: April 3, 2004

2004 Chief Albert John Luthuli (posthumous)
Former President, African National Congress
Recipient, Nobel Peace Prize, 1960
Venue: Durban Institute of Technology—Durban, South Africa
Date: July 30, 2004

2005 Rabbi Michael Lerner Editor, *Tikkun* Magazine
Founder and National Cochair
The Tikkun Community
Rabbi, Beyt Tikkun
Venue: Morehouse College—Atlanta, Georgia
Date: March 31, 2005

2005 Mr. John Hume
Architect, Northern Ireland Peace Settlement
Founder and Former Leader, Social Democratic and Labour Party
Corecipient, Nobel Peace Prize, 1998
Venue: Queens University—Belfast, Northern Ireland
Date: October 27, 2005

2006 Archbishop Desmond M. Tutu
Anglican Archbishop Emeritus of Cape Town
Recipient, Nobel Peace Prize, 1984

Venue: Morehouse College—Atlanta, Georgia
Date: January 26, 2006

2006 Mrs. Coretta Scott King (posthumous)
First Lady of Civil Rights
Founder, The Martin Luther King Jr. Center for Nonviolent
    Social Change
Leader, The Effort to Make Dr. King's Birthday a National Holiday
Venue: Morehouse College—Atlanta, Georgia
Date: April 6, 2006

2009 Mr. Yitzhak Rabin (posthumous)
Prime Minister, State of Israel
Architect, Oslo Accords
Corecipient, Nobel Peace Prize, 1994
Venue: Morehouse College—Atlanta, Georgia
Date: April 2, 2009

2010 Dr. Han Shik Park
University Professor of Interational Affairs;
Director, Center for the Study of Global Issues, (GLOBIS)
    University of Georgia
Architect of US–North Korean Relations
Venue: Morehouse College—Atlanta, Georgia
Date: April 1, 2010

2011 Rev. Dr. Joseph Echols Lowery
Dean of the American Civil Rights Movement
Cofounder and President, Southern Christian
    Leadership Conference (SCLC)

Mrs. Evelyn Gibson Lowery
Pioneer, American Civil Rights Movement
Founder, The SCLC/Women's Organizational (shared prize)
Movement for Equality Now Inc. (WOMEN)
Venue: Morehouse College—Atlanta, Georgia
Date: April 24, 2011

2013 His Holiness Sri Sri Ravi Shankar
Founder, Art of Living Foundation
Founder, International Association for Human Values
Global Ambassador of Peace, Humanitarian, and Spiritual Leader
Venue: Morehouse College—Atlanta, Georgia
Date: April 3, 2013

2014 Dr. Karen Armstrong
Founder, Charter for Compassion
Leading Historian of World Religion, Thinker, Bestselling Author
Venue: Morehouse College—Atlanta, Georgia
Date: April 3, 2014

2015 Ambassador Anwarul K. Chowdhury
United Nations Under-Secretary-General
President, UNICEF Board and Permanent Representative to the
    UN for Bangladesh
Venue: Morehouse College—Atlanta, Georgia
Date: April 9, 2015

2016 Dr. Johan Galtung
Father of International Peace and Conflict Studies
Founder, Galtung Institute for Peace Theory and Peace Practice
Founder, TRANSCEND International
Venue: Morehouse College—Atlanta, Georgia
Date: April 5, 2016

2017 Brother James Gaffney, FSC
President Emeritus and Honorary Founder, Lewis University
Venue: Morehouse College—Atlanta, Georgia
Date: March 30, 2017

2018 Dr. Neelakanta Radhakrishnan
Director Emeritus, Gandhi Smriti and International Center
    of Gandhian Studies
Venue: Morehouse College—Atlanta, Georgia
Date: April 5, 2018

Appendix B

Gandhi, King, Ikeda: A Legacy of Building Peace Exhibition Venues*

Gandhi, King, Ikeda Award Recipients

The Ohio State University—Columbus, Ohio (5/16/01)

Mr. Amos H. Lynch
Publisher/CEO, the *Columbus Post*

Dr. William E. Kirwan
President, The Ohio State University

Mr. Theodore S. Celeste
Former member of the Ohio House of Representatives

Rev. Otha Gilyard
Senior Minister, Shiloh Baptist Church

University of Saint Maarten—Saint Maarten (5/28/01)

Dr. Josianne Fleming-Artsen
Director, University of St. Maarten

Hon. Denzel Douglas
Prime Minister, Saint Kitts & Nevis

Lewis University—Romeoville, Illinois (6/2/01)

Brother James Gaffney
President, Lewis University

All venues attended by Lawrence Edward Carter Sr.

Roosevelt University—Chicago, Illinois (6/19/01)

Dr. Theodore L. Gross
President, Roosevelt University

Mr. Lerone Bennet Jr.
Executive Editor, *Ebony* Magazine

Riverside Church—New York, New York (7/15/01)

Rev. Dr. James A. Forbes
Senior Minister, The Riverside Church

Hon. Rev. Floyd Flake
Pastor, Allen A.M.E. Church

Dr. Vincent L. Wimbush
Professor, Union Theological Seminary

Atlanta Community Center—Riverdale, Georgia (8/5/01)

Dr. N. Radhakrishnan
Director, Gandhi Smriti and International Center of
    Gandhian Studies

SCLC Annual Convention—Montgomery, Alabama (8/5/01)

No Gandhi, King, Ikeda Awards conferred

University of Rhode Island—Kingston, Rhode Island (8/10/01)

Ambassador Andrew Young
Former US Ambassador to the United Nations

Mr. Lincoln C. Almond
Governor, Rhode Island

Dr. Robert L. Carothers
President, University of Rhode Island

Rev. Dr. Bernard LaFayette
Professor, University of Rhode Island

Dr. Virgil Woods
Professor, University of Rhode Island

Dr. Elise Boulding
Professor Emeritus, Dartmouth University

Soka University of America, Aliso Viejo, California
No Gandhi, King, Ikeda Awards conferred

University of Missouri—Columbia, Missouri (10/29/01)

Dr. John C. Schuder
Peace activist and University Professor Emeritus

Mr. Bill Wickersham
President, Friends of Peace Studies

California State University, Los Angeles—Los Angeles, California (1/10/02)

Dr. James M. Rosser
President, California State University, Los Angeles

Columbus Metropolitan Library—Columbus, Ohio (1/19/02)

State Rep. Ray Miller
State House of Representatives, Ohio

Dr. Gene Thomas Harris
Superintendent, Columbus, Ohio, Public Schools

Rev. William Guernesy Barndt
Pastors for Peace, Columbus, Ohio

Martin Luther King Jr. Birthday Breakfast—Columbus, Ohio (1/21/02)

Hon. Michael B. Coleman
Mayor, Columbus, Ohio

AGAPE International Spiritual Center—Culver City, California (1/30/02)

Rev. James M. Lawson
Civil rights pioneer and Pastor, Holman United Methodist Church

Ms. Barbara Fields Bernstein
Executive Director, Association for Global New Thought

Rev. Dr. Michael Bernard Beckwith
Founder, Agape International Center

Ms. Ricky Byars Beckwith
Music Director, Agape International Center

Ms. Eisha Mason
Executive Director, Center for the Advancement of Nonviolence

Michigan State University—East Lansing, Michigan (3/25/02) MSU Union

Mrs. Rosa Parks
Rosa and Raymond Parks Institute for Self-Development

Mr. M. Peter McPherson, JD
President, Michigan State University

Rev. Dr. Charles Gilchrist Adams
Pastor, Hartford Memorial Baptist Church

Dr. E. Sharon Banks
Superintendent, Lansing School District

Rev. Argentina Glasgow
Senior Minister, Detroit Unity Temple

Dr. Robert L. Green
Civil rights pioneer and Professor, Michigan State University

Rev. Dr. Jim Holley
Pastor, The Holistic Little Rock Baptist Church

Rev. James Connelle Perkins
Pastor, Greater Christ Baptist Church

Rev. Dr. Carlyle Fielding Stewart
Pastor, Hope United Methodist Church

Martin Luther King Jr. International Chapel, Morehouse College—Atlanta, Georgia (4/4/02)

Imam Warith Deen Mohammed
Muslim American Society, Chicago, Illinois

University of California, Berkeley—Berkeley, California (4/27/02)

Dr. Robert M. Berdahl
Chancellor, University of California, Berkeley

Rev. Dr. Lauren Artress
Canon, Grace Cathedral

Rev. Dr. Amos C. Brown
Senior Pastor, Third Baptist Church

Rev. Dr. Matthew Fox
President, University of Creation Spirituality

Rev. Eloise Oliver
Minister, East Bay Church of Religious Science

Rev. J. Alfred Smith
Senior Pastor, Allen Temple Baptist Church

Rev. Joan Steadman
Senior Minister, First Church of Religious Science

Right Rev. William Edwin Swing
Episcopal Bishop, Diocese of California

Rev. Cecil Williams
Minister, Glide Memorial United Methodist Church

Soka University—Tokyo, Japan (9/12/02)

Ambassador Aftab Seth
Ambassador to Japan, Government of India

"Aloha Peace Concert," Neal S. Blaisdell Center—Honolulu, Hawaii (9/14/02)

Dr. Evan S. Dobelle
President, University of Hawaii

Hon. Dr. Neil Abercrombie
US Representative, Hawaii (1st District)

University of Chicago—Chicago, Illinois (10/4/02)

Dr. Don Michael Randel
President, University of Chicago

Stephan P. Clark County Building—Miami-Dade County, Florida (12/13/02)

Ms. Lida Rodriguesz-Taseff
President, American Civil Liberties Union

Dr. Barbara Carey-Shuler
Chairperson, Miami-Dade Commission

Dr. Robert Ingram
Vice Chair, Miami-Dade School Board

Rev. Fritz Bazin
Dean, North Dade Diocese of Southeast Florida

Mr. Pedro Armando Freyre
Vice Chair, Miami-Dade Community Relations Board

Mr. Ahmed Kabani
Board member, Miami-Dade Community Relations Board

Martin Luther King Jr. Birthday Celebration, West Covina, California (1/20/03)

Hon. Hilda L. Solis
US Representative, California (32nd District)

Princeton University—Princeton, New Jersey (2/3/03)

Ms. Heddye Brinson Ducree
Director, Carl A. Fields Center for Equality and Cultural
Understanding, Princeton University

Dr. Peter J. Paris
Professor, Princeton Theological Seminary Past President,
American Academy of Religion

Dr. Richard O. Hope
Vice President, Woodrow Wilson National Fellowship
Foundation Visiting Professor, Princeton University

Rev. Robert Moore
Executive Director, Coalition for Peace Action

Rev. Moses William Howard
Pastor, Bethany Baptist Church, Newark, New Jersey

Dr. Mark Lewis Taylor
Professor, Princeton Theological Seminary

Rev. Dr. Joseph C. Williamson
Retired Dean of Religious Life and of the Chapel, Princeton
University

University of Minnesota—Minneapolis, Minnesota (2/22/03)

Mr. Jim Anderson
Cultural Cochair and Historian, Mendota Mdewakanton
Dakota Native American Community

Dr. David Vassar Taylor
Dean, General College, University of Minnesota

Ms. Amal Yusuf
Chief Executive, Somalian Women's Association

Metro Hall, City of Toronto—Toronto, Canada (4/7/03)

Hon. Lincoln M. Alexander
Chancellor, University of Guelph
Fmr. Minister of Labor, Canada, and Fmr. Lieut. Governor, Ontario

Dr. Ursula Franklin
Professor Emeritus, University of Toronto

Hon. Douglas Roche
Appointed to the Senate of Canada (Alberta)
Former Ambassador for Disarmament, Canada

Parliament of New Zealand—Wellington, New Zealand (7/29/03)

Mr. Tohu Kakahi (posthumous)
19th-century Maori leader for nonviolent action

Mr. Te Whiti o Rongomai
(posthumous)
19th-century Maori leader for nonviolent action

Dr. Ian A.M. Prior
Chairperson, International Physicians for the Prevention of
   Nuclear War (New Zealand); Principal, World Court Project

Hon. Sonja Davies, MP (ret.)
Member, Parliament (Ret.- Pencarrow)
Social and peace activist

New Zealand Cultural Center—Auckland, New Zealand (8/3/03)

Hon. Grahame William Hall
Mayor, District of Rotorua and Justice of the Peace

Berlin City Hall—Berlin, Germany (9/20/03)

Dr. Horst-Eberhard Richter
Cofounder and Honorary Board Member, International
   Physicians for the Prevention of Nuclear War (Germany)

M.K. Gandhi Annual Birthday Banquet—Edmonton, Alberta, Canada (10/2/03)

The Hon. Lois Elsa Hole, CM
Lieutenant Governor, Province of Alberta, Canada

Club of Rome Annual Meeting—Amman, Jordan (10/07/03)

H.E. Abdel Salam Majali, MD
Former Prime Minister, The Kingdom of Jordan

H.E. Adnan Badran, PhD
President, Philadelphia University in Jordan

Ms. Samar Kildani
Director, El Hassan Youth Award

National Library—Roseau, Commonwealth of Dominica (11/06/03)

Hon. Pierre Charles
Prime Minister, The Commonwealth of Dominica

Concordia University—Montreal, Quebec, Canada (11/10/03)

Dr. Frederick Lowy
Rector and Vice Chancellor, Concordia University

Ms. Monique Mujawamariya
Founder and Deputy Chairperson, Fonds Africa

Annual Meeting of the Coalition of California Black School Board Members—San Diego, California (12/12/03)

Ms. Ernestine Jones
Board member and Former President, Governing Board of the
San Ysidro Schools

Ms. Gwen Estes
Board member, New Haven-Union City School District
Member, Anti-Hate Crime Task Force, Alameda County

Stanford University—Palo Alto, California (01/23/04)

Dr. Clayborne Carson
Professor of History, Stanford University
Director, Martin Luther King Jr. Papers Project

Hon. LaDoris Hazzard Cordell
Vice Provost for Campus Relations and Special Counselor to the
    President, Stanford University
Councilwoman, Palo Alto City Council

Rev. William L. McLennan
Dean of Religious Life, Stanford University

**Vision Theater, City of Los Angeles—Los Angeles,
California (02/06/04)**

Hon. James K. Hahn
Mayor, City of Los Angeles

Denver University—Denver, Colorado (03/01/04)

Dr. Maria Guajardo Lucero
Director, Mayor's Office of Education and Children,
    City of Denver

Prof. Ved Prakash Nanda
Vice Provost, Office of Internationalization
Director, International Legal Studies Program,
    University of Denver

San Jose State University—San Jose, California (04/23/04)

Hon. Susan Hammer
Former Mayor, City of San Jose

Ms. Delorme McKee-Stovall
Acting Director, Office of Human Relations County of
    Santa Clara

University of California, Los Angeles—Los Angeles, California (05/12/04)

Ms. Dolores Huerta
Cofounder, United Farm Workers of America
Former Regent, University of California

Dr. Winston Churchill Doby
Vice President for Educational Outreach, University of California

Los Angeles Southwest College—Los Angeles, California (05/13/04)

Hon. Mark Ridley-Thomas
Assemblyman, 48th District, California State Assembly

Ms. Dianna M. Newton
President, El Centro School Board, El Centro, California

Santa Monica College—Santa Monica, California (05/13/04)

Mr. Tommie Smith
Gold Medalist, Men's 200 Meter Sprint, 1968 Olympics
Director, Athletic Department, Santa Monica College

University of Sydney—Sydney, Australia (06/15/04)

Mrs. Stella Cornelius, AO, OBE
Director, Conflict Resolution Network

Griffith University—Brisbane, Australia (06/17/04)

Mrs. Joan Shears
Peace worker and social activist

University of Melbourne—Melbourne, Australia (06/18/04)

Ms. Lillian Holt
Vice Chancellor's Fellow, University of Melbourne
Former Principal, Tauondi Aboriginal College

Curtin University—Perth, Australia (06/21/04)

Ms. Marie Joan Winch
Adjunct Professor, Curtin University
Founder, Aboriginal Marr Moodij "Good Hands" Health
    Education Program

Museum Africa—Johannesburg, South Africa (08/03/04)

No Gandhi, King, Ikeda Awards conferred

**World Council of Churches Assembly—Atlanta, Georgia
(10/04/04)**

No Gandhi, King, Ikeda Awards conferred

The University of Guelph—Ontario, Canada (10/19/04)

Hon. Lloyd Axworthy, PhD
President and Vice Chancellor, The University of Winnipeg
Fmr. Minister of Foreign Affairs (1996–2000), Canada

Chatham College—Pittsburgh, Pennsylvania (11/05/04)

Dr. Esther L. Barazzone
President, Chatham College

Mr. Melvin Carnell Blount
Cornerback, Pittsburgh Steelers (1970–1984)
1989 Inductee, Pro Football Hall of Fame
Founder, Mel Blount Youth Home

Dr. Anne Fields-Ford
Adjunct Associate Professor of Social Work, The University of
    Pittsburgh

San Carlos National Museum—Mexico City, Mexico (11/16/04)

Ms. Beatriz Pages Rebollar
General Director and Publisher, Revista *Siempre!*

Yale University—New Haven, Connecticut (01/28/05)

Dr. Elsie Watson Cofield
Founder and President, AIDS Interfaith Network

Rev. Dr. Samuel Nathaniel Slie
Associate Pastor, Church of Christ in Yale, Battell Chapel,
  Yale University

Morehouse College—Atlanta, Georgia (03/31/05)

Rev. Theodore Judson Jemison
Pioneer, Baton Rouge Bus Boycott Movement
President Emeritus, National Baptist Convention, USA Inc.
Morehouse College Trustee

Kennesaw State University—Kennesaw, Georgia (04/8/05)

No Gandhi, King, Ikeda Awards conferred

**Virginia Polytechnic Institute and State University—
Blacksburg, Virginia (04/11/05)**

Ms. Susan Gayle Anderson
Instructor, Dept. of Mathematics, Virginia Tech
Student activities advisor, human rights activist

**Neighborhood USA National Convention, Sacramento
Convention Center—Sacramento, California (05/26/05)**

No Gandhi, King, Ikeda Awards conferred

**National Underground Railroad Freedom Center—
Cincinnati, Ohio (12/01/05)**

Hon. Marian Spencer
Former Deputy Mayor and Former member, Cincinnati
  City Council
Civil rights pioneer

Dr. Steve Sunderland
Professor, Peace Studies, University of Cincinnati
Peace activist and counsellor

University of Cincinnati—Cincinnati, Ohio (02/24/06)

Dr. Paul Eric Abercrumbie
Adjunct Associate Professor of African American Studies
Director, African American Culture and Research Center
Founder, Black Man Think Tank

University of Southern California, Los Angeles—Los Angeles, California (03/24/06)

Mr. Joe Adams
Entertainment industry pioneer
Airman, Tuskegee Airmen Fighter Group
Benefactor to 25 Adams Scholars at Morehouse College

Boston University—Boston, Massachusetts (04/19/06)

Dr. Charles J. Ogletree Jr.
Jesse Climenko Professor of Law
Associate Dean for the Clinical Programs
Founding and Executive Director
Charles Hamilton Houston Institute for Race and Justice
Harvard Law School

University of North Florida—Jacksonville, Florida (09/18/06)

Mr. Stetson Kennedy
Author, folklorist, human rights activist, environmentalist,
    and KKK infiltrator

Dr. Michael Aaron Hallett
Professor and Chair, Dept. of Criminology and Criminal Justice
Director, Center for Race and Juvenile Justice Policy
The University of Northern Florida

Hampton University—Hampton, Virginia (10/02/06)

Dr. William R. Harvey
President, Hampton University

Wisma Kebudayaan Soka Gakkai Malaysia—Kuala Lumpur, Malaysia (10/19/06)

Dr. Datuk Jemilah Mahmood
President, Malaysian Medical Relief Society (MERCY Malaysia)

Tanjung Bunga Beach Hotel—Penang, Malaysia (10/21/06)

Mr. Dato' Anwar Fazal, JP, DJN
Chairperson, Taiping Peace Initiative and the Malaysian
   Interfaith Network
Regional Coordinator, Asia Pacific 2000 UNDP
Global consumer rights and public health advocate

Black Cultural Centre For Nova Scotia—Dartmouth, Nova Scotia, Canada (11/11/06)

Dr. Bridglaí Pachai
Professor of History (Ret)
Executive Director, Black Cultural Centre of Nova Scotia
Executive Director, Nova Scotia Human Rights Commission

Dr. Henry Vernon Bishop, Hon.D.
Chief Curator, Black Cultural Centre For Nova Scotia

University of Michigan—Ann Arbor, Michigan (01/12/07)

Ms. Rose Anita Hunt Redd
Executive Vice President, Citizens for Progressive Change

Hofstra Universiy—Hempstead, New York (02/02/07)

Mr. Frederick Kevin Brewington
Civil rights attorney

Mr. Martin Melkonian
Adjunct Associate Professor of Economics, Hofstra University

Mr. Margaret Melkonian
Vice President and UN Representative, Hague Appeal for Peace
(joint award)

Washington University—St. Louis, Missouri (04/16/07)

Ms. Judy Ann Bentley, MA, RNC
President and Chief Executive, Community Health-in-
  Partnership Services (CHIPS)

**Harrisburg Area Community College—Harrisburg,
Pennsylvania (10/02/07)**

Dr. Edna Victoria Baehre
President, Harrisburg Area Community College

Dr. Nevers Sekwila Mumba
Former Vice President, Republic of Zambia

**University of California, Merced—Merced, California
(10/12/07)**

Dr. Sung-Mo "Steve" Kang
Chancellor and Professor of Engineering, University of
  California, Merced

Phoenix City Hall—Phoenix, Arizona (12/07/07)

Pearl Mao Tang, MD
Former Director, Maricopa County Bureau of Maternal
  and Child Health

Hon. Thomas Tang, LLB
Judge, 9th US Circuit Court (posthumous)
(joint award)

Hon. Calvin Coolidge Goode
Former member, City Council, Phoenix Arizona

University of Maryland—College Park, Maryland (05/05/08)

Dr. Joanne Mitchell Martin
Founder and President, National Great Blacks in Wax Museum Inc.

Dr. Elmer Perry Martin
Founder, National Great Blacks in Wax Museum Inc.
(posthumous) (joint award)

Allen County Public Library—Fort Wayne, Indiana (09/20/08)

Rev. Dr. Terry Anderson
Senior Pastor, First Presbyterian Church
Fmr. Executive Director, The Samaritan Counseling Center
Fmr. Associate Director, The Associated Churches

University of Indiana Northwest—Gary, Indiana (10/20/08)

Dr. Bruce Bergland
Chancellor, University of Indiana Northwest

University of Nevada, Las Vegas—Las Vegas, Nevada (02/05/09)

Hon. Steven Alexander Horsford
Democrat, Clark County Senatorial District No. 4
Majority Leader, Nevada State Senate
President of the Board of Trustees, Nevada Partners

Mr. Tony F. Sanchez, III
Corporate Senior Vice President, Public Policy & External
 Affairs, Nevada Energy
Vice President of the Board of Trustees, Nevada Partners

Salt Lake City Public Library—Salt Lake City, Utah (05/03/09)

Hon. Ross C. "Rocky" Anderson
Former Mayor, Salt Lake City, Utah
Founder and Executive Director, High Road for Human Rights

Jeju National University—Jeju Island, Republic of Korea (05/12/09)

Dr. Cho Moon-Boo
President, Jeju National University (1997–2001)

Professor Emeritus and Professor of Political Science
Jeju National University

Louisiana State Captiol, Senate Chamber—Baton Rouge, Louisiana (09/27/09)

Hon. Sharon Weston Broome
Senator and President Pro Tempore, Louisiana State Senate
President, National Organization of Black Elected Legislative
    Women

Pennsylvania State University—State College, Pennsylvania (10/28/09)

Dr. Graham Spanier
President, Pennsylvania State University

DePaul University—Chicago, Illinois (01/18/10)

The Monsignor John J. Egan Urban Center
The Irwin W. Steans Center for Community-Based Service
    Learning & Community Service Studies

San Diego State University—San Diego, California (02/05/10)

Dr. Murugappa C. Madhavan
Professor of Economics and Asian Studies Emeritus, San Diego
State University
Founder, Mahatma Gandhi Scholarship and Memorial Lecture

Carleton University—Ottawa, Ontario, Canada (10/01/10)

Hon. John Edward Broadbent
Member of the Canadian Parliament, 1968–1989, 2006–2008
Leader, New Democratic Party, 1975–1989
President, International Centre for Human Rights and
Democratic Development

**Rosa Parks Museum and Library, Troy University—
Montgomery, Alabama (10/15/10)**

Dr. Fred David Gray
American Civil Rights lawyer and pioneer
Attorney for Rosa Parks, Montgomery Bus Boycott, Attorney for
Tuskegee Syphilis Study participants

**International Civil Rights Museum (Woolworth's)—
Greensboro, North Carolina (10/15/10)**

Hon. Yvonne J. Johnson
Former Mayor, City of Greensboro
Executive Director, One Step Further Inc.

**University of Washington, Tacoma—Tacoma,
Washington (01/18/11)**

Dr. Michael K. Honey
Fred T. and Dorothy G. Haley Endowed
Professor of the Humanities
Professor of Labor and Ethnic Studies and American History
University of Washington, Tacoma

Morehouse College—Atlanta, Georgia (01/25/11)

Dr. Vincent Gordon Harding
Civil rights pioneer and scholar
Professor Emeritus of Religion and Social Transformation
Iliff School of Theology, Denver, Colorado

Coppin State University—Baltimore, Maryland (04/26/11)

Dr. Calvin W. Burnett
Former President, Coppin State University, 1972–2003
Cofounder and Past President, The Black/Jewish Forum of
  Baltimore (BLEWS)

Mr. Bernard L. Berkowitz
Fmr. President and CEO, Baltimore Economic Development
  Corporation (BEDCO)
Treasurer and Past President, The Black/Jewish Forum of
  Baltimore (BLEWS)

Konyang University—Nonsan, Korea (09/28/11)

Dr. Hi-Soo Kim
Founder and President, Konyang University
Founder, Konyang University Hospital

**Coady International Institute, St. Xavier University—
Antigonish, Nova Scotia, Canada (10/07/11)**

Dr. Michael Aubrey Edwards
Distinguished Senior Fellow, Demos
Senior Visiting Fellow, Brooks World Poverty Institute,
  University of Manchester

Christ Unity Church—Sacramento, California (01/14/12)

Rev. Michael Moran
Founder and Senior Minister of Worship
Spiritual Life Center—Sacramento

University of South Florida—Saint Petersburg, Florida (03/20/12)

Mr. William Edwards
Chairman and CEO, Mortgage Investors Corporation

Pukyong National University—Busan, Korea (05/09/12)

Dr. Maeng Eon Park
President, Pukyong National University

North American College—Houston, Texas (04/08/13)

Mr. Cherry Steinwender
Founder and Executive Director, Center for the Healing of Racism

Boise State University—Boise, Idaho (02/03/14)

Hon. Cherie Buckner-Webb
Senator, Idaho State Legislature
Founding Board member, Idaho Black History Museum

Columbine High School—Littleton, Colorado (03/17/14)

Mr. Frank DeAngelis
Principal, Columbine High School

Northwest Florida State College—Niceville, Florida (08/16/14)

Rev. H. K. Matthews
Pioneer of the American Civil Rights Movement
Champion of peace and justice, Pensacola, Florida

Dr. Clifford Dale Herron
Founding Executive Director, Mattie Kelly Fine & Performing
    Arts Center, Northwest Florida State College

Martin Luther King Jr. Birthday Breakfast—Phoenix, Arizona (12/5/14)

Rev. Dr. Paul Eppinger
Statewide Director, Arizona "Victory Together" Campaign
Executive Director, Arizona Interfaith Movement

Morehouse College—Atlanta, Georgia (04/09/15)

Imam Fetullah Gulen
Turkish Muslim thinker, author, poet, opinion leader, and
educational activist

Parliament of the World's Religions—Salt Lake City, Utah (10/14/15)

No Gandhi, King, Ikeda Awards conferred

Morehouse College—Atlanta, GA (3/31/16)

Dr. Mohamed Keshavjee
Lawyer, mediator, trainer
Global specialist on family mediation

Morehouse College—Atlanta, GA (3/30/17)

No Gandhi, King, Ikeda Awards conferred

Morehouse College—Atlanta, Georgia (4/5/18)

Dr. Peter Ackerman
Founding Chair of the International Center on Nonviolent Conflict

Appendix C

Annual Peace Proposals Delivered by Daisaku Ikeda to the Member Ambassadors of the General Assembly of the United Nations each January 26, SGI Day

See www.daisakuikeda.org for more information

2018—Toward an Era of Human Rights: Building a People's Movement

2017—The Global Solidarity of Youth: Ushering in a New Era of Hope

2016—Universal Respect for Human Dignity: The Great Path to Peace

2015—A Shared Pledge for a More Humane Future: To Eliminate Misery From the Earth

2014—Value Creation for Global Change: Building Resilient and Sustainable Societies

2013—Compassion, Wisdom and Courage: Building a Global Society of Peace and Creative Coexistence

2012—Human Security and Sustainability: Sharing Reverence for the Dignity of Life

2011—Toward a World of Dignity for All: The Triumph of the Creative Life

2010—Toward a New Era of Value Creation

2009—Toward Humanitarian Competition: A New Current in History

2008—Humanizing Religion, Creating Peace

2007—Restoring the Human Connection: The First Step to Global Peace

2006—A New Era of the People: Forging a Global Network of Robust Individuals

2005—Toward a New Era of Dialogue: Humanism Explored

2004—Inner Transformation: Creating a Global Groundswell for Peace

2003—A Global Ethic of Coexistence: Toward a "Life-Sized" Paradigm for Our Age

2002—The Humanism of the Middle Way: Dawn of a Global Civilization

2001—Creating and Sustaining a Century of Life: Challenges for a New Era

2000—Peace Through Dialogue: A Time to Talk, Thoughts on a Culture of Peace

1999—Toward a Culture of Peace: A Cosmic View

1998—Humanity and the New Millennium: From Chaos to Cosmos

1997—New Horizons of a Global Civilization

1996—Toward the Third Millennium: The Challenge of Global Citizenship

1995—Creating a Century Without War Through Human Solidarity

1994—Light of the Global Spirit: A New Dawn in Human History

1993—Toward a More Humane World in the Coming Century

1992—A Renaissance of Hope and Harmony

1991—Dawn of the Century of Humanity

1990—The Triumph of Democracy: Toward a Century of Hope

1989—Toward a New Globalism

1988—Cultural Understanding and Disarmament: The Building Blocks of World Peace

1987—Spreading the Brilliance of Peace Toward the Century of the People

1986—Dialogue for Lasting Peace

1985—New Waves of Peace Toward the Twenty-First Century

1984—A World Without War

1983—New Proposals for Peace and Disarmament

Appendix D

A List of Daisaku Ikeda's Published Dialogues

source: www.daisakuikeda.org

1. *Bunmei nishi to higashi* (Civilization, east and west) with Richard Coudenhove-Kalergi. Japanese (1972).
2. *On the Japanese Classics* with Makoto Nemoto. English, Japanese (1974), Portuguese, Thai.
3. *Choose Life: A Dialogue* with Arnold J. Toynbee. Bengali, Bulgarian, Chinese (traditional), Czech, Dutch, English, Filipino, French, German, Hindi, Hungarian, Indonesian, Italian, Japanese (1975), Korean, Laotian, Malay, Nepali, Polish, Portuguese, Russian, Serbian, Sinhalese, Spanish, Swahili, Thai, Turkish, Urdu.
4. *Jinsei mondo* (On living) with Konosuke Matsushita. Chinese (traditional), Chinese (simplified), Korean, Japanese (1975).
5. *Ningen kakumei to ningen no joken* (Changes within: Human revolution vs. human condition) with André Malraux. Japanese (1976).
6. *Letters of Four Seasons* with Yasushi Inoue. Chinese (simplified), English, French, Japanese (1977), Malay, Thai.
7. *Dawn After Dark* with René Huyghe. Chinese (simplified), English, French (1980), Japanese, Portuguese, Spanish, Thai.

8. *Before It Is Too Late* with Aurelio Peccei. Bulgarian, Chinese (traditional), Chinese (simplified), Danish, English, French, German, Indonesian, Italian, Japanese (1984), Korean, Malay, Portuguese, Spanish, Swedish, Thai, Vietnamese.

9. *Human Values in a Changing World* with Bryan Wilson. Chinese (traditional), Chinese (simplified), English, French, Italian, Japanese (1985), Portuguese, Spanish, Thai.

10. *Dai san no niji no hashi* (The third rainbow bridge) with Anatoli A. Logunov. Chinese (simplified), Japanese (1987), Russian.

11. *Heiwa to jinsei to tetsugaku o kataru* (Philosophy of human peace) with Henry Kissinger. Japanese (1987).

12. *Humanity at the Crossroads* with Karan Singh. English, Japanese (1988), Thai.

13. *Search for a New Humanity* with Josef Derbolav. Chinese (simplified), English, German (1988), Japanese, Thai.

14. *A Lifelong Quest for Peace* with Linus Pauling. Chinese (traditional), Chinese (simplified), English, Filipino, French, Japanese (1990), Korean, Malay, Russian, Spanish, Vietnamese.

15. *Tonko no kosai* (The radiance of Dunhuang: On beauty and life) with Chang Shuhong. Chinese (traditional), Chinese (simplified), Japanese (1990).

16. *Sekai shimin no taiwa* (Dialogue between citizens of the world) with Norman Cousins. Japanese (1991).

17. *Taiyo to daichi: Kaitaku no uta* (The sun and the good earth: An ode to pioneering Japanese immigrants) with Ryoichi Kodama. Japanese (1991), Kyrgyz, Portuguese.

18. *Ode to the Grand Spirit* with Chingiz Aitmatov. English, German, Japanese (1991), Kyrgyz, Russian.

19. *Ningen to bungaku o kataru* (Dialogue on humanity and culture) with Kenji Doi. Japanese (1991).

20. *Space and Eternal Life* with Chandra Wickramasinghe. English, Japanese (1992), Portuguese.

21. *Kagaku to shukyo* (Science and religion) with Anatoli A. Logunov. Japanese (1994), Russian.

22. *Human Rights in the Twenty-First Century* with Austregésilo de Athayde. English, Japanese (1995), Portuguese.

23. *Choose Peace* with Johan Galtung. English, Italian, Japanese (1995), Korean, Thai.

24. *Moral Lessons of the Twentieth Century* with Mikhail Gorbachev. Chinese (traditional), Chinese (simplified), English, French, German, Greek, Icelandic, Italian, Japanese (1996), Korean, Russian, Slovakian.

25. *Taiheiyo no kyokujitsu* (Dawn of the Pacific) with Patricio Aylwin Azócar. Japanese (1997), Spanish.

26. *Haranbanjo no Naporeon* (The tempestuous life of Napoleon) with Philippe Moine, Patrice Morlat, and Tadashige Takamura. Japanese (1997).

27. *Compassionate Light in Asia* with Jin Yong. Chinese (traditional), Chinese (simplified), English, Japanese (1998).

28. *Kodomo no sekai* (The path to the land of children) with Albert A. Likhanov. Chinese (traditional), Chinese (simplified), Japanese (1998), Russian.

29. *Utsukushiki shishi no tamashii* (A lion's heart) with Axinia Djourova. Bulgarian, Japanese (1999).

30. *On Being Human: Where Ethics, Medicine, and Spirituality Converge* with René Simard and Guy Bourgeault. Chinese (traditional), English, French, Italian, Japanese (2000).

31. *Global Civilization: A Buddhist-Islamic Dialogue* with Majid Tehranian. Arabic, Chinese (traditional), Dutch, English, French, Indonesian, Italian, Japanese (2000), Malay, Persian, Thai.

32. *José Martí, Cuban Apostle* with Cintio Vitier. English, Japanese (2001), Spanish.

33. *Choose Hope* with David Krieger. English, Italian, Japanese (2001).

34. *Distinct Encounters* with Rogelio M. Quiambao. English, Japanese (2001).

35. *Sekai no bungaku o kataru* (Dialogue on world literature) with Tadashige Takamura and Philippe Moine; Kentaro Nishihara and Rogelio M. Quiambao; Ryohei Tanaka and Hirotomo Teranishi; Tadashige Takamura and Henry Indangasi. Japanese (2001).

36. *Atarashiki jinrui o atarashiki sekai o* (Beyond the century: Dialogue on education and society) with Victor A. Sadovnichy. Chinese (traditional), Japanese (2002), Russian.

37. *Toyo no chie o kataru* (Dialogue on oriental wisdom) with Ji Xianlin and Jiang Zhongxin. Chinese (traditional), Chinese (simplified), Japanese (2002).

38. *Buddhism: A Way of Values* with Lokesh Chandra. English, Korean, Japanese (2002).

39. *Kibo no seiki e takara no kakehashi* (The bridge toward a century of hope) with Cho Moon Boo. Korean, Japanese (2002).

40. *Planetary Citizenship* with Hazel Henderson. Chinese (simplified), Chinese (traditional), English, French, Italian, Japanese (2002), Portugese.

41. *Gaku wa hikari: Bunmei to kyoiku no mirai o kataru* (The illuminating power of learning) with Victor A. Sadovnichy. Chinese (traditional), Japanese (2004).

42. *Uchu to chikyu to ningen* (The cosmos, earth, and human beings) with Alexander Serebrov. Japanese (2004), Korean, Russian.

43. *Ningen to bunka no niji no kakehashi* (A rainbow bridge of humanity and culture) with Cho Moon Boo. Japanese (2005).

44. *Our World To Make: Buddhism and the Rise of Global Civil Society* with Ved Prakash Nanda. English, Japanese (2005).

45. *Ningenshugi no dai seiki o* (Toward creating an age of humanism) with John Kenneth Galbraith. Japanese (2005).

46. *A Dialogue Between East and West: Looking to a Human Revolution* with Ricardo Díez-Hochleitner. English, Japanese (2005), Malay, Spanish.

47. *Into Full Flower: Making Peace Cultures Happen* with Elise Boulding. English, Japanese (2006).

48. *Revolutions: To Green the Environment, to Grow the Human Heart* with M. S. Swaminathan. English (2005), Italian, Japanese, Vietnamese.

49. *A Quest for Global Peace* with Joseph Rotblat. Chinese (traditional), English, German, Italian, Japanese (2006).

50. *Creating Waldens: An East-West Conversation on the American Renaissance* with Ronald A. Bosco and Joel Myerson. English, Japanese (2006).

51. *New Horizons in Eastern Humanism: Buddhism, Confucianism, and the Quest for Global Peace* with Tu Weiming. Chinese (traditional), Chinese (simplified), English, Japanese (2007).

52. *The Humanist Principle: On Compassion and Tolerance* with H.C. Felix Unger. English, Japanese (2007).

53. *A Passage to Peace: Global Solutions from East and West* with Nur Yalman. English, Japanese (2007).

54. *Yujo no daisogen* (Grand steppes of friendship) with Dojoogiin Tsedev. Japanese (2007), Mongolian.

55. *The Persistence of Religion: Comparative Perspectives on Modern Spirituality* with Harvey Cox. Chinese (traditional), English, Japanese (2008).

56. *Walking with the Mahatma: Gandhi for Modern Times* with Neelakanta Radhakrishnan. English, Chinese (traditional), Japanese (2009), Malayalam, Tamil.

57. *Bunka to geijutsu no tabiji* (A journey on the path of vulture and the arts) with Jao Tsung-I. Chinese (traditional), Chinese (simplified), Japanese (2009).

58. *Tenmongaku to buppo o kataru* (A dialogue on astronomy and Buddhism) with Ronaldo Rogério de Freitas Mourão. Chinese (traditional), Japanese (2009), Portuguese.

59. *Jinken no seiki e no messeiji* (A message to the century of human rights) with Adolfo Pérez Esquivel. Italian, Japanese (2009), Spanish.

60. *Asu o tsukuru kyoiku no seigyo* (Shaping the future: The sacred task of education) with Hans Henningsen. Danish, Japanese (2009).

61. *Kyoiku to bunka no odo* (The noble path of education and culture) with Chang Jen Hu. Chinese (traditional), Japanese (2010).

62. *The Wisdom of Tolerance: A Philosophy of Generosity and Peace* with Abdurrahman Wahid. English, Indonesian, Japanese (2010).

63. *Ningen shori no shunju: Rekishi to jinsei to kyoiku o kataru* (An epoch of human triumph: A dialogue on history, life, and education) with Zhang Kaiyuan. Chinese (traditional), Chinese (simplified), Japanese (2010).

64. *The Inner Philosopher: Conversations on Philosophy's Transformative Power* with Lou Marinoff. Chinese (simplified), English, Italian, Japanese (2011).

65. *Heiwa no ashita e kyoiku no taiko: Ukuraina to nihon no yujo* (The great light of education toward the dawn of peace: Ukraine–Japan friendship) with Michael Z. Zgurovsky. Japanese (2011), Russian, Ukrainian.

66. *Atarashiki chikyu shakai no sozo e: Heiwa no bunka to kokuren o kataru* (Creating a new global society: A discourse on the United Nations and a culture of peace) with Anwarul K. Chowdhury. Chinese (traditional), Japanese (2011).

67. *Nijuisseiki no Naporeon: Rekishi sozo no esupuri (seishin) o kataru* (Napoleon of the twenty-first century: A conversation on the spirit of creating history) with Charles Napoléon. Japanese (2011).

68. *Chikyu o musubu bunkaryoku* (Connecting the world through the power of culture) with Gao Zhanxiang. Chinese (simplified) (2012), Japanese.

69. *Heiwa no kakehashi: Ningen kyoiku o kataru* (Humanistic education: A bridge to peace) with Gu Mingyuan. Chinese (simplified), Japanese (2012).

70. *America Will Be!: Conversations on Hope, Freedom, and Democracy* with Vincent Harding. English, French, Japanese (2012).

71. *Reaching Beyond: Improvisations on Jazz, Buddhism, and a Joyful Life* with Herbie Hancock and Wayne Shorter. English, Japanese (2013).

72. *Asu no sekai, kyoiku no shimei: Nijuisseiki no ningen o kosatsu suru* (The mission of education in tomorrow's world: Thoughts on humanity in the twenty-first century) with Victor Sadovnichy. Japanese (2013).

73. *The Art of True Relations: Conversations on the Poetic Heart of Human Possibility* with Sarah Wider. English, Japanese (2013).

74. *Living As Learning: John Dewey in the Twenty-First Century* with Jim Garrison and Larry Hickman. English, Japanese (2014).

75. *Heiwa no tetsugaku to shigokoro o kataru* (A conversation on the philosophy of peace and the poetic spirit) with Stuart Rees. Japanese (2014).

76. *Knowing Our Worth: Conversation on Energy and Sustainability* with Ernst Ulrich von Weizsäcker. English, German, Italian, Japanese (2014).

77. *Inochi no hikari haha no uta* (The light of life: Songs of mothers) with Jutta Unkart-Seifert. Japanese (2015).

78. *Global Citizenship: Toward a Civilization of Wisdom, Love, and Peace* with José Veloso Abueva. English, Japanese (2015).

79. *Arata na gurobaru shakai no shihyo* (Shaping a new society: Discussions on peace in the twenty-first century) with Lawrence J. Lau. Chinese (traditional), Japanese (2015).

80. *Aratana chikyu bunmei no uta o: Tagoru to sekai shimin o kataru* (Song for a new global civilization: On Tagore and world citizens) with Bharati Mukherjee. Japanese (2016).

81. *Heiwa no seiki e: Minshu no chosen* (Toward a century of peace: A dialogue on the role of civil society in peace-building) with Kevin Clements. Japanese (2016).

82. *Mirai ni okuru jinsei tetsugaku* (A life philosophy for the future) with Wang Meng. Japanese (2017).

Notes

Preface

1. Martin Luther King Jr., "The American Dream," in *A Testament of Hope: The Essential Writings and Speeches of Martin Luther King Jr.*, ed. James M. Washington (New York: HarperCollins, 1991), 210.

2. John 10:16 (Revised Standard Version).

3. Rajmohan Gandhi, *Gandhi: The Man, His People, and the Empire* (Berkeley: University of California Press, 2007), 241.

Chapter One: Getting the Call

4. Martin Luther King Jr., *Where Do We Go From Here? Chaos or Community* (Boston: Beacon Press, 2010), 177.

5. Arnold Toynbee and Daisaku Ikeda, *Choose Life*, ed. Richard L. Gage (Oxford: Oxford University Press, 1976), 200–1.

6. A week later a second gathering took place in the chapel library, and I was shocked that one person in the room had traveled from Tokyo, Japan. The second meeting included Danny Nagashima, Ian McIlraith, Yoshi Nagaoka, Cliff Sawyer, Richard Brown, and Brad Yeates.

7. Martin Luther King Jr., "Letter from Birmingham City Jail," in *A Testament of Hope: The Essential Writings and Speeches of Martin Luther King Jr.*, ed. James M. Washington (New York: HarperCollins, 1991), 290.

8. Daisaku Ikeda, *Life: An Enigma, A Precious Jewel,* trans. Charles S. Terry (Tokyo: Kodansha, 1983), 209–10.

9. Ikeda, *Life: An Enigma,* 210.

Chapter Two: My Path

10. Daisaku Ikeda, *Hope Is a Decision* (Santa Monica, CA: Middleway Press, 2017), 48.

Chapter Three: Meeting My Mentor

11. Samuel Dubois Cook, ed., *Benjamin E. Mays, His Life, Contribution, and Legacy* (Franklin, TN: Providence House, 2009), 87.

12. Martin Luther King Jr., "The American Dream," in *A Testament of Hope: The Essential Writings and Speeches of Martin Luther King Jr.,* ed. James. M. Washington (New York: HarperCollins, 1991), 209.

13. King, *A Testament of Hope,* 211.

14. King, *A Testament of Hope,* 211-12.

15. King, *A Testament of Hope,* 214.

16. Martin Luther King Jr., "A Knock at Midnight," in *Strength to Love* (New York: Harper and Row, 1963), 42.

Chapter Four: Turning Poison Into Medicine

17. John D. Godsey, "Bonhoeffer's Costly Theology," *Christian History,* no. 32. https://christianhistoryinstitute.org/magazine/article/bonhoeffers-costly-theology.

18. See Mark 10:31 and Luke 13:30 (Revised Standard Version).

19. Matthew 5:17 (King James Version).

20. Luke 23:43 (Revised Standard Version).

Chapter Five: Morehouse Mission

21. The Augusta Institute became the Atlanta Baptist Seminary in 1879. The seminary became the Atlanta Baptist College in 1897, which in turn was named Morehouse College in 1913.

22. *The Papers of Martin Luther King Jr.*, ed. Clayborne Carson (Los Angeles: University of California Press, 1992), 1:1–9.

23. Matthew 20:26–28 (Revised Standard Version).

Chapter Six: World House

24. Martin Luther King Jr., "Letter from Birmingham City Jail," in *A Testament of Hope: The Essential Writings and Speeches of Martin Luther King Jr.*, ed. James M. Washington (New York: HarperCollins, 1991), 297.

25. Mark 3:33 and 35 (New Revised Standard Version).

26. John 10:16 (King James Version).

27. Kenneth L. Smith and Ira G. Zepp Jr., *Search for the Beloved Community: The Thinking of Martin Luther King Jr.* (Valley Forge, PA: Judson Press, 1974), 119.

28. Smith and Zepp, *Beloved Community*, 119.

29. Smith and Zepp, *Beloved Community*, 120.

30. Smith and Zepp, *Beloved Community*, 120.

31. Martin Luther King Jr., *Where Do We Go From Here? Chaos or Community* (Boston: Beacon Press, 2010), 181.

Chapter Seven: Human Revolution

32. Elaine Pages, *The Origin of Satan* (New York: Random House, 1996), xvii.

Chapter Eight: Buddhist Teacher

33. Daisaku Ikeda, *My Recollections* (Santa Monica, CA: World Tribune Press, 1980), 40.

34. Olivier Urbain, ed., *A Forum for Peace: Daisaku Ikeda's Proposals to the UN* (London: I.B. Tauris, 2014), 540.

35. Matthew 6:10 (Revised Standard Version).

Chapter Nine: The Power of Moral Cosmopolitan Dialogue

36. According to the June 2016 Gallup Poll. Percentage of people who trust Congress, 9 percent; organized labor, 23 percent; the criminal justice system, 23 percent; the presidency, 36 percent; church or organized religion, 41 percent; the police, 56 percent; the military; 73 percent.

Chapter Eleven: Value Creation

37. Matthew 22:37 (King James Version).

38. Letter to Charles Yancey, January 6, 1816. https://founders. archives.gov/documents/Jefferson/03-09-02-0209.

Chapter Twelve: Global Commonwealth of Realized Citizens

39. Daisaku Ikeda, *A New Humanism* (London: I.B. Tauris, 2010), 192.

40. Daisaku Ikeda, "Toward a Culture of Peace: A Cosmic View." https://www.sgi-usa.org/newsandevents/docs/peace1999.pdf.

41. Daisaku Ikeda, "The Flowering of the Greater Self." Message to the Ikeda Center for Peace, Learning, and Dialogue regarding the publication of *Creating Waldens: An East-West Conversation on the American Renaissance.* http://www. ikedacenter.org/20th-anniversary/ikeda-messages/2009.

42. Daisaku Ikeda, *The Human Revolution* (Santa Monica, CA: World Tribune Press, 2004), viii.

43. Martin Luther King Jr., "A Christmas Sermon on Peace," in *A Testament of Hope: The Essential Writings and Speeches of Martin Luther King Jr.*, ed. James Melvin Washington (New York: HarperCollins, 1991), 253.

44. Ikeda, *A New Humanism*, 55.

Chapter Thirteen: An Inside Job

45. Luke 17:21 (King James Version).

46. Paul Elie, *The Life You Save May Be Your Own* (New York: Farrar, Straus, and Giroux, 203), 413.

47. Elie, *The Life You Save*, 413.

48. Daisaku Ikeda, et. al., *The Wisdom of the Lotus Sutra* (Santa Monica, CA: World Tribune Press, 2000), 1:14.

49. John 14:12 (Revised Standard Version).

50. Martin Luther King Jr., "Loving Your Enemies." https://
kinginstitute.stanford.edu/king-papers/documents/lov-
ing-your-enemies-sermon-delivered-dexter-avenue-bap-
tist-church.

51. King, "Loving Your Enemies." https://kinginstitute.stanford.
edu/king-papers/documents/loving-your-enemies-ser-
mon-delivered-dexter-avenue-baptist-church.

52. Daisaku Ikeda, *The Human Revolution* (Santa Monica, CA:
World Tribune Press, 2004), viii.

53. Daisaku Ikeda, *A New Humanism* (London: I.B. Tauris,
2010), 231.

54. Martin Luther King Jr., "The American Dream," in *A
Testament of Hope: The Essential Writings and Speeches of
Martin Luther King Jr.*, ed. James M. Washington (New York:
Harper Collins, 1991), 210.

Chapter Fourteen: Faith to Heal the World

55. *Hamlet*, Act 5, Scene 2.

56. Daisaku Ikeda, *The Living Buddha* (Santa Monica, CA:
Middleway Press, 2008), ix.

57. Olivier Urbain, ed., *A Forum for Peace: Daisaku Ikeda's
Proposals to the UN* (London: I.B. Tauris, 2014), 78.

58. *Forum for Peace*, 11.

59. Ralph Waldo Emerson, *The American Scholar* (New York:
The Laurentian Press, 1901), 31.

60. Martin Luther King Jr., "The Sword That Heals," *The Critic*,
21, no. 6 (June–July 1964).

61. From The Ethics of International Engagement and
Service-Learning Project website: http://ethicsofisl.ubc.
ca/?s=ethical+pluralism.

62. Martin Luther King Jr., "Letter from Birmingham City Jail," in *A Testament of Hope: The Essential Writings and Speeches of Martin Luther King Jr.*, ed. James M. Washington (New York: HarperCollins, 1991), 302.

63. *Forum for Peace*, 292–93.

64. Matthew 8:5–10 (King James Version).

Selected Bibliography

Azaransky, Sarah. *This Worldwide Struggle, Religion and the International Roots of the Civil Rights Movement.* New York: Oxford University Press, 2017.

Bertocci, Peter A. *The Goodness of God.* Washington, D.C.: University Press of America, 1981.

Carson, Clayborne, ed. *The Papers of Martin Luther King Jr.* Vol. 1, *Called to Serve: January 1929–June 1951,* edited by Ralph E. Luker and Penny A. Russell. Berkeley: University of California Press, 1992.

Carter, Lawrence Edward Sr. "A Cosmo Vision for a Common Future: Becoming Moral Cosmopolitan Humanists in the Global Village, the WorldHouse, the International Solidarity of Peace-Loving Nations, and the Global Commonwealth of Citizen (VHSC) Gandhi, King-Mandela, Ikeda." In *Global Visioning: Hopes and Challenges for a Common Future (Peace and Policy 19),* edited by Oliver Urbain and Ahmed Abaddi. New York: Routledge, 2017.

———. "Growing Up Into Democracy's Crown." Address at the dedication ceremonies of Soka University of America, Aliso Viejo, CA, May 4, 2001.

———, ed. *Walking Integrity.* Macon, GA: Mercer University Press, 1998.

Chomsky, Noam. *Who Rules the World?* New York: Metropolitan Books, 2016.

Dooley, Tom. *Deliver Us From Evil.* New York: Farrar, Straus, and Cudahy, 1956.

Holmes, Ernest. *The Science of Mind*. New York: Penguin Putnam, 1938.

———. *Words That Heal Today*. Deerfield Beach, FL: Health Communications Inc., 1949.

Ikeda, Daisaku. *Faith Into Action*. Santa Monica, CA: World Tribune Press, 1999

———. *The Heart of the Lotus Sutra*. Santa Monica, CA: World Tribune Press, 2013.

———. *The Human Revolution*. 6 vols. Boulder, CO: Weatherhill Inc., 1972–99.

———. *Life: An Enigma, a Precious Jewel*. New York: Kodansha International, 1982.

———. *A New Humanism: The University Addresses of Daisaku Ikeda*. London: I.B. Tauris, 2010.

———. *Unlocking the Mysteries of Birth and Death*. Santa Monica, CA: Middleway Press, 2003.

———. Katsuji Saito, Takanori Endo, and Haruo Suda. *The Wisdom of the Lotus Sutra*. 6 vols. Santa Monica, CA: World Tribune Press, 2000–03.

Kang, Namsoon. *Cosmopolitan Theology: Reconstituting Planetary Hospitality Neighbor-Love, and Solidarity in an Uneven World*. Saint Louis: Chalice Press, 2013.

Kapur, Sudarshan. *Raising Up a Prophet: The African-American Encounter With Gandhi*. Boston: Beacon, 1992.

King Jr., Martin Luther. *Where Do We Go From Here? Chaos or Community*. Boston: Beacon Press, 1967.

———. "A Knock at Midnight." In *Strength to Love*. New York: Harper and Row, 1963.

———. "A Time to Break Silence." In *A Testament of Hope: The Essential Writings and Speeches of Martin Luther King Jr.*, edited by James M. Washington. New York: HarperCollins, 1991.

———. "A Christmas Sermon on Peace." In *A Testament of Hope: The Essential Writings and Speeches of Martin Luther King Jr.*, edited by James M. Washington. New York: HarperCollins, 2003.

———. "I Have a Dream." In *I Have A Dream*. San Francisco: Harper, 1992.

———. Dexter Avenue Baptist Church sermon, 1957.

McIntosh, Steve. *Integral Consciousness and the Future of Evolution*. St. Paul, MN: Paragon House, 2007.

Neville, Robert Cummings. *Boston Confucianism: Portable Tradition in the Late-Modern World*. Albany, NY: State University of New York Press, 2000.

Nichiren. *The Writings of Nichiren Daishonin*. 2 vols. Translated by the Gosho Translation Committee. Tokyo, Japan: Soka Gakkai, 2003–06.

Nix Jr., Echol, ed. *In The Beginning, The Martin Luther King Jr. International Chapel at Morehouse College*. Macon, GA: Mercer University Press, 2015.

Pagels, Elaine. *The Origin of Satan*. New York: Vintage Books, 1996.

———. *The Gnostic Gospels*. New York: Vintage Books, 1989.

Ricoeur, Paul. *Lectures on Ideology and Utopia*. Edited by George H. Taylor. New York: Columbia University Press, 1986.

Smith, Kenneth and Ira Zepp. *Search for the Beloved Community: The Thinking of Martin Luther King Jr.* Valley Forge, PA: Judson Press, 1974.

Strand, Clark. "Born in the USA: Racial Diversity in Soka Gakkai International." *Tricycle: The Buddhist Review*. Winter 2003.

———. *Waking the Buddha: How the Most Dynamic and Empowering Buddhist Movement in History Is Changing Our Concept of Religion*. Santa Monica, CA: Middleway Press, 2014.

Thurman, Howard. *For the Inward Journey: The Writings of Howard Thurman.* Selected by Anne Spencer Thurman. New York: Harcourt Brace Jovanovich, 1984.

Toynbee, Arnold and Daisaku Ikeda. *Choose Life: A Dialogue.* Edited by Richard L. Gage. New York: Oxford University Press, 1976.

Urbain, Olivier. *Daisaku Ikeda's Philosophy of Peace, Dialogue, Transformation and Global Citizenship.* New York: I.B. Tauris, 2011.

———, ed. *A Forum for Peace: Daisaku Ikeda's Proposals to the UN.* London: I.B. Tauris, 2014.

Wilber, Ken. *Integral Spirituality: A Startling New Role for Religion in the Modern and Postmodern World.* Boston: Integral Books, 2007.

Index

About the Preacher and the Teacher

The Preacher

In 1958, Martin Luther King Jr. privately recruited **LAWRENCE EDWARD CARTER SR.** as a tenth grader to come to Morehouse College. Twenty-one years later, in 1979, Carter became the founding dean of the Martin Luther King Jr. International Chapel at Morehouse, the world's largest religious memorial to the legacy of the great civil rights leader, whose mission is to teach, encourage, and inspire ambassadors of King's beloved world community. He is also chairman of the Howard Thurman Educational Trust.

Carter has spent his career working to realize King's vision for peace and justice through education and action, including lectures at universities and seminaries around the world.

Born in Dawson, Georgia, and reared in Columbus, Ohio, he graduated from Virginia University of Lynchburg with a BA in social science and psychology before studying at Boston University, where he earned his MDiv degree in theology, the STM degree in pastoral care, and a PhD in pastoral psychology and counseling. He is also a professor of religion at Morehouse and a Baptist minister. He has one son, Carter, and lives in Stonecrest, Georgia, with his wife, Marva.

The Teacher

DAISAKU IKEDA is a peacebuilder, Buddhist philosopher, educator, author, and poet. He was president of the Soka Gakkai lay Buddhist organization in Japan from 1960 to 1979 and is the founding president of the Soka Gakkai International, one of the world's largest and most diverse community-based Buddhist associations, promoting a philosophy of empowerment and social engagement for peace. He is also the founder of the Soka schools system and several international institutions promoting peace, culture, and education.

Ikeda is a strong proponent of dialogue as the foundation of peace. Since the 1970s he has pursued dialogue with individuals from diverse backgrounds—prominent figures from around the world in the humanities, politics, faith traditions, culture, education, and various academic fields—in order to discover common ground and identify ways of tackling the complex problems facing humanity.

Ikeda is a prolific writer who has published more than 250 works, ranging from commentaries on Buddhism to biographical essays, poetry, and children's stories. He has two sons, Hiromasa and Takahiro, and lives with his wife, Kaneko, in Tokyo.